DANISH YEARBOOK
OF
PHILOSOPHY

VOLUME 40

DANISH YEARBOOK
OF
PHILOSOPHY

VOLUME 40

2005

MUSEUM TUSCULANUM PRESS
UNIVERSITY OF COPENHAGEN 2006

Published for
Dansk Filosofisk Selskab
in cooperation with
the Philosophical Societies of Aarhus and Odense
and with financial support from
the Danish Research Council for the Humanities

*

*

Articles for consideration and all editorial communications should be sent in three copies to:
Danish Yearbook of Philosophy
University of Copenhagen, Department of Philosophy
Njalsgade 80, DK 2300 Copenhagen S, Denmark

Business communications, including subscriptions and orders for reprints, should
be addressed to the publishers:
MUSEUM TUSCULANUM PRESS
Njalsgade 94
DK 2300 Copenhagen S
Denmark

*

© 2006 DANISH YEARBOOK OF PHILOSOPHY
COPENHAGEN, DENMARK
PRINTED IN DENMARK
BY SPECIAL-TRYKKERIET · BYENS TRYK A-S

ISBN 87-635-0494-4
ISSN 0070-2749

CONTENTS

The contributions from Christine Korsgaard, Dick Howard and Jean-Luc Marion were delivered, in slightly different forms, as keynote speeches in Copenhagen at the Annual Meeting 2005 of the Danish Philosophical Society. The contribution from Peter Kemp was delivered as an introductory address at the same event.

Christine Korsgaard's contribution also appears in *Studies in Practical Reason*, edited by V. Bradley Lewis, from Catholic University Press, and in *The Constitution of Agency: Studies in Practical Reason and Moral Psychology*, by Christine M. Korsgaard, from Oxford University Press. Jean-Luc Marion's contribution has previously appeared in the *Graduate Faculty Philosophy Journal*, published by the Department of Philosophy, New School for Social Research, New York. It is reprinted here with the permission of that journal.

Danish Yearbook of Philosophy, Vol. 40 (2005), 7-10

THE NEW ENLIGHTENMENT

Peter Kemp

Professor of Philosophy,
Department of the Philosophy of Education,
Danish University of Education

The Enlightenment is the name of an important era in European history, the 18th Century, when philosophers, writers, artists and other intellectuals thought that the time had come for free thinking to develop. The Enlightenment is therefore also tied to the concept of emancipation, of liberation from authoritarian traditions and institutions, or "man's emergence from his self-incurred immaturity", self-incurred because of his lack of resolution and courage to use his reason without the guidance of another (as Immanuel Kant says in his article "An Answer to the question: 'What is Enlightenment?'" from 1784)[1].

But the Enlightenment was also a programme of education, of bringing about a better understanding of human being's world and life through both a better theoretical and a better practical understanding than traditional authorities had brought to people. The Enlightenment contains the metaphor of light. The aim of the Enlightenment is to bring the light of free reason to everyone. This is the transmission of the light of insight.

In French Enlightenment is called *Les lumières,* the lights, but this word has not, unlike the English word Enlightenment, retained the full meaning of the German word *Aufklärung. Aufklärung* is the process of coming to an understanding, not an understanding of an already established knowledge. Kant explained it in these words: "If it is now asked whether we at present live in an enlightened age (*in einem aufgeklärten Zeitalter*), the answer is: No, but we do live in an age of enlightenment (*in einem Zeitalter der Aufklärung*)". As things are at present, Kant argues, we still have a long way to go before human beings (*die Menschen*) as a whole can use their own reason "free from outside direction"[2].

You might say that the idea of Enlightenment is still important because this process has not ended and is still necessary. However, do we not live in an age of communication where all kinds of information are readily accessible? In this time of the internet never before has it been so easy to find information, to acquire knowledge about all kinds of subjects. Yes, but at the same time we are manipulated by the media, by seductive politicians, by spin-doctors, by lies or "half-truths" in advertising, so that our interpretations of information still are guided by manipulators. Moreover, forces such as pressure, censorship, marginalization and the like prevent people from expressing their own opinions. In many societies imprisonment, death threats, executions and assassinations occur frequently. It is thus really an academic question to discuss if our time is more enlightened than in the 18th century.

Consequently, we should not say that the Enlightenment is still relevant for us as philosophers *because* the process of free insight has not come to an end, but we should rather say that it is an urgent matter *because* we must start again and again the project of the Enlightenment.

Many of the leading philosophers of our time have expressed this urgency. Let me only mention the late Jacques Derrida, who passed away on October 16, 2004. He was often called a post-modern thinker because he criticised the modern belief in pure reason. He wanted – as for instance Adorno and Horkheimer – to get beyond an Enlightenment that destroyed freedom in the name of knowledge and repressed poetry, imagination, and dreams by reducing them to entertainment and replaced insight from experience with pure technical rationality.

See, for instance, his conference from 1998: *University without condition* [3]. Here Derrida speaks about the task of the university and especially of philosophy. This task is twofold – to search for the truth professionally and to confess this involvement. It can be said briefly in French: "L'université *fait profession* de la vérité"[4], "fait profession" = perform a profession and make a confession. And Derrida explains this practice of the university in the following way: "It (the university) claims, it promises an engagement without limits to the truth" ("un engagement sans limite envers la vérité").

By emphasizing such an engagement Derrida focused on the resolution and courage that Kant saw as the necessary condition for enlightenment. Kant did not consider the immaturity that the Enlightenment should overcome as a tragic fate, but rather as a self-incurred state. The motto of the Enlightenment was therefore: "*Sapere Aude!* Have courage to use your *own* reason".

Thus, the Enlightenment includes the concept of critique in the modern sense, which does not mean rejection but rather an approach to the understanding of conditions of knowledge, of poetic imagination, of social life, and thereby an understanding of science, literature, art, life, ethics and law – a true understanding of mankind.

Enlightenment, however, is not only a theoretical project, but also, and mainly, a practical project, a social project. This social project is expressed in the idea of tolerance. The ethical goal of the Enlightenment is attaining the good life in society, the good society with peace between citizens and between societies. Therefore conflicts between religions were the main problem for the philosophers. Let me only mention two philosophers who made proposals for solving the problem with the idea of tolerance: Pierre Bayle and Jean-Jacques Rousseau.

Both made a sharp distinction between moral (norms) and religious convictions. Bayle declared in his *Commentaire philosophiques sur ces paroles de Jésus Christ "Contrains les entrer"* (1686-87), that insight into what is good and bad does not arise from religious dogmas, but rather from intuitions in human consciousness. And Rousseau claimed that religion is subordinate to social life. He speaks in *The Social Contract* (1762) about *la religion civile,* the civil religion, which differs from Christ proclaiming a kingdom that is not of this world. Further, in *Emile* (in the same year) Rousseau claims a religious education that is a formation of the heart by ideas that come from the inner voice of reason. Thus, according to this idea of tolerance in Bayle and Rousseau, only so called "natural religion" (a Western idea of the natural) should be tolerated.

But as Derrida shows in his dialogue with Giovanna Borradori a few weeks after September 11, 2001, this idea of tolerance is an idea that is always on the side of "the reason of the strongest" where "might is right"[5]. You could also say, as Herbert Marcuse said in the sixties, that it is repressive tolerance.[6] Derrida moreover argues that it is not "pure and unconditional hospitality, hospitality *itself*", since this hospitality "opens or is in advance open to someone who is neither expected nor invited, to whomever arrives as an absolute foreign visitor, as a new arrival, non-identifiable and non-foreseeable, in short, wholly other"[7]. Here Derrida speaks of course of our Western attitude to foreigners, Muslims, Chinese, or Africans whom we tolerate, but on our own conditions.

This means that to revive the project of the Enlightenment is not simply to repeat it, but to recreate it, so that we search for the truth without repressing others in the name of this truth. Thus we have to recreate the idea of tolerance so that tolerance does not mean contempt for the religious convictions of others but on the contrary, recognition of the importance of these convictions. Then we can tolerate religious differences, not because religious convictions have no real influence in ethics and politics, but because they are crucial motivating factors or are themselves deep motives of ethics and politics.

Similarly we cannot simply apply the idea of practical reason in the Enlightenment and in particular in Kant. In his *Groundwork of the Metaphysics of Moral*s the concept of respect – *Achtung* – plays a crucial role as the only acceptable feeling, and this respect only focuses on the moral law, not on the person as such. Therefore, Kant can argue that "any respect for a person is properly only respect for the law"[8] (Acad. Ed. 4.402, note). Thus, it is European rationality that is the object of respect; I cannot respect the other if he or she does not think the moral law as I think it.

But this correction of Kant's morality can invoke the idea in Kant of a republican contract not only between citizens of an individual society but also between all human beings. According to this cosmopolitan contract every human being – every *Mensch* – counts as a member of humanity, and according to Kant himself we can speak of the *hospitality* that we have to practice according to the cosmopolitan law, *das Weltbürgerrecht.*

Perhaps we should say, that to perform enlightenment today is to recognize the right to existence in every member of mankind, even a human being whose morals we cannot respect. So even a terrorist, to whose action and ideas we cannot pay deference, should not be placed in a camp such as Guantanamo and should not be deprived of all human rights.

Notes

1. Immanuel Kant: "Beantwortung der Frage: Was ist Aufklärung?", *Kant's gesammelte Schriften,* Akademie Ausgabe, Band VIII, Berlin, 1912, S. 33-42; English translation: "What is Enlightenment?" in *On History,* edited by Lewis White Beck, The Library of Liberal Arts, Macmillan, New York/London, 1963, p. 3-10.
2. *Ibid.* S. 40; engl. transl. p. 8-9.
3. Jacques Derrida: *L'Université sans condition*, Galilée, Paris, 2001.
4. *Ibid.,* p. 12.
5. Giovanna Borradori : *Philosophy in the Time of Terror, Dialogues with Jürgen Habermas and Jacques Derrida*, The University of Chicago Press, Chicago, 2003, p. 127.
6. Herbert Marcuse: "Repressive Tolerance" in *A Critique of Pure Tolerance*, Cape Editions, reprinted 1971., Boston, 1965.
7. *Philosophy in the Time of Terror,* p. 128-129.
8. Immanuel Kant. *Grundlegung zur Metaphysik der Sitten, Kant's gesammelte Schriften,* Akademie Ausgabe, Band IV, Berlin, 1903, S. 402 note **; engl. transl: *Groudwork of the Metaphysic of Morals,* Translated by H.J.Paton, Harper Torchbooks, Harper and Row, New York/London, 1964, p. 69, note **.

Danish Yearbook of Philosophy, Vol. 40 (2005), 11-36

ACTING FOR A REASON[1©]

CHRISTINE M. KORSGAARD

Harvard University

Forthcoming in *Studies in Practical Reason*, edited by V. Bradley Lewis, from Catholic University Press and in *The Constitution of Agency: Studies in Practical Reason and Moral Psychology*, by Christine M. Korsgaard, from Oxford University Press.

I. Introduction: Reason and Reasons

The question I am going to discuss is what a practical reason is: that is, what we are referring to when we talk about "the reason for an action," and what happens when someone acts for a reason. The answer I am going to present is one that I believe is common to Aristotle and Kant, and that distinguishes them from nearly everyone else. I am also going to suggest that their answer is correct, for an important reason. As I will try to explain, the view I believe we find in Aristotle and Kant enables us to connect their account of what *reasons* are with an important feature of their account of what *Reason* is: namely, that Reason is in a particular way the *active* aspect or dimension of the mind.

More generally, when we talk about reason, we seem to have three different things in mind. In the philosophical tradition, reason refers to the active rather than the passive or receptive aspect of the mind. Reason in this sense is opposed to perception, sensation, and perhaps emotion, which are forms of or at least involve undergoing. The contrast is not unproblematic, for it seems clear that receptivity itself cannot be understood as wholly passive. The perceived world does not merely enter the mind, as through an open door. In sensing and responding to the world our minds interact with it, and the activity of our senses themselves makes a contribution to the character of the perceived world. Though at some level innate and automatic, this contribution may be shaped and extended by learning, changed by habituation and experience, and perhaps even consciously directed. But the mental activity that we associate with reason goes beyond that involved in even the most sophisticated receptivity. Reasoning is self-conscious, self-directing activity through which we deliberately give shape to the inputs of receptivity. This happens both in the case of theoretical reasoning, when we are constructing a scientific account of the world, and in the case of practical reasoning, where its characteristic manifestation is choice.

Reason has also traditionally been identified with either the employment of, or simply conformity to, certain principles, such as the principles of logical inference, the principles Kant identified as principles of the understanding, mathematical principles, and the principles of practical reason. A person is called reasonable or rational when his beliefs and actions conform to the dictates of those principles, or when he is deliberately guided by them. And then finally, there are the particular considerations, counting in favor of belief or action, that we call "reasons."

The use of the English word "reason" in all of these contexts, and the way we translate equivalent terms from other languages, suggests a connection, but what exactly is it? Aristotle and Kant's conception of what practical reasons are, I believe, can help us to answer this question, by bringing out what is distinctive, and distinctively active, about acting for a reason. That, at least, is what I am going to argue.

II. Three Questions about Reasons

There are actually three, or at least three, questions about the ontology of reasons for action. The first question is what sorts of items count as reasons for action – in particular, whether reasons are provided by our mental states and attitudes, or by the facts upon which those states and attitudes are based. (I'll explain this contrast in greater detail below.) The second question is what kinds of facts about actions are relevant to reasons, and in particular whether reasons always spring from the goals achieved through action or sometimes spring from other properties of the actions, say that the action is just or kind. This question is most familiar to us from the debate between consequentialists and deontologists. The third question is how reasons for action are related to actions themselves, and in particular whether this relation is to be understood causally or in some other way.[2] Put in more familiar terms, this is the question what we mean when we say that someone is "motivated."

How do we answer these questions? Most philosophers would agree that practical reasons have at least some of the following properties: (1) They are normative, that is, they make valid claims on those who have them. (2) They are motivating, that is, other things equal, the agents who have them will be inspired to act in accordance with them.[3] And (3) they are motivating in virtue of their normativity, that is, people are inspired to do things by the normativity of the reasons they have for doing them, by their awareness that some consideration makes a claim on them. I will call this property being "normatively motivating," and, although it is not uncontroversial, I am inclined to assume that this is what is what a practical reason should essentially be: a normatively motivating consideration. We answer questions about the ontology of reasons by asking whether our candidate items could possibly have the properties in question, and by keeping our eye on the connection between Reason and reasons.

The first question – whether reasons are provided by mental states or by the facts upon which those states are based – leads to a problem, which I will call the problem of the reflexive structure of reasons, and which I will describe in the next section. I will then show how Aristotle and Kant's view solves that problem, by the way that it answers the second question, about whether the value of actions rests in their consequences or elsewhere. Finally in the last section I will say a little about the question how reasons and actions are related, the question of motivation.

III. Mental States and Good-making Properties

Bernard Williams once wrote: "Desiring to do something is of course a reason for doing it."[4] Joseph Raz disagrees. "Wants … are not reasons for action," he writes. "The fact that [actions] have a certain value – that performing them is a good thing to do because of the intrinsic merit of the action or of its consequences – is the paradigmatic reason for action."[5] The debate about whether reasons are provided by mental states or by facts about the value of the actions arises in part because our ordinary practice of offering reasons seems to go both ways. Suppose I ask: "Why did Jack go to Chicago?" Sometimes we offer as the answer some mental state of Jack's. We might say "he wanted to visit his mother," for instance. The mental state might be a desire, as in the example I have just quoted, or it might be a belief. "He believed his mother needed his help." Many philosophers, of course, think that the reason is given by a belief/desire pair. For instance, he wanted to visit his mother, and believed that she was to be found in Chicago; or, he wanted to help his mother, and believed that he could help her by going to Chicago. On that showing, the answers I gave earlier are partial, offered on the assumption that the questioner can easily work out the rest for herself. When I reply "he wanted to visit his mother," for instance, I leave the questioner to conclude that he believed his mother was to be found in Chicago.

But philosophers like Raz insist that, despite the fact that we answer questions in this way, the reason is not given by Jack's mental states, but rather by certain facts that those mental states are a response to: facts about what I will call the good-making properties of the actions. An important caveat here: I do not mean by using the phrase "good-making properties" to prejudge the question whether agents always act for the sake of what they regard as good in any moral or substantial sense.[6] I am using the term 'good' here to refer to whatever it is about the action that makes it seem eligible to the agent. If St. Augustine is right, then the badness of an action may be one of its good-making properties in the formal sense in which I am using the term.[7] We can still ask whether what gave the young Augustine a reason to steal those famous pears is the fact that the action is bad or his desire to do something bad. The defenders of the view that good-making properties are reasons will say that it is the *fact* that the action is bad, not his desire to do the bad. After all, these philosophers urge, reasons are things that agents act *on*. The agent is confronted by the reason, and the reason makes a kind of claim on him, it calls out to him that a certain action is to be done, or at least is eligible to be done. So we should identify as reasons the kinds of items that first-person deliberators take to be reasons, the kind of items that play a role in deliberation. And – leaving Augustine and returning to the more benign Jack – unless Jack is really a very self-absorbed character, what he takes to make a claim on him are not his own mental states, but what's good about the action he proposes to do. After all, if you ask Jack why he is going to Chicago, it would a bit odd for him to say, "because I want to." He might of course say "Because I want to help my mother," but according to the defenders of good-making properties, we should not take this formulation to express the idea that his desire is his reason, for he could equally say, with exactly the same force, "Because my mother needs my help." Certainly it seems likely that when he talks to *himself* about the situation, and decides what to do, he talks to himself about his mother and her troubles, not about his own mental states. So if he does say "I am going because I want to help my mother," instead of taking that to mean that his desire is his reason, we should take it as a kind of announcement that he thinks he both has, *and is responding to*, a reason. Here he describes his response to the reason as a want, a desire. But he could equally well, or perhaps even better, say "I *need* to help my mother," or "I *have to* help my mother" where "need" or "have to" refers not merely to a psychological state (or not to a *merely psychological* state), but to a normative response – something along the lines of "I feel that I am under an obligation to help my mother."

But the view that the reasons are given by the good-making properties of the proposed actions also runs into certain objections. For there seem to be problems about saying that the (supposedly) good-making properties of action, all by themselves, can be normative or motivating. For one thing, there are the standard objections to normative realism. Objectors to realism insist that facts and natural properties by themselves (such as the fact that an action would help one's mother) are normatively inert. And for another, there are problems about explaining motivation and the sense of obligation by appeal to the good-making properties of actions alone. After all, people who are aware of the good-making properties of action sometimes fail to be motivated by them or to acknowledge that they present any sort of normative claim. For the good-making properties of actions to have normative and motivational effects, to exert a claim on the agent in light of which he acts, there must be a certain uptake: the agent must *take* them to be good-making properties and be moved accordingly. And the defender of mental states will argue that when someone fails to respond to the good-making properties in question, we can identify what we would need to *add* in order to provoke the response. To the person who is not motivated by his mother's need for help we might add a desire to help her. To the person who finds no normative claim associated with helping his mother, we might add the belief that one ought to help one's family. And in this way we seem to come back around to the view that reason-giving force arises at least in part from the agent's mental states after all.

But the defender of good-making properties will deny this. The problem I just described, he will say, only arises from a shift in standpoint. When we talk third-personally about the fact that an agent did or did not respond to the reasons before him, we talk about his mental states, since those constitute the responses in question. But that doesn't mean that the mental states are part of the reason, or that they play any role in the agent's own deliberations. The good-making properties of the action provide the reason, and to say that the agent desires to help or feels himself obliged to help is only to say that he is responding appropriately to the good-making properties of helping. After all, if the good-making properties have no motivating or normative force on their own – if we have to *add* the mental states, in order to get the motivating or normative force – then someone who lacks the mental states in question will quite properly be unmoved by the supposedly good-making properties. But surely we *do* want to say that there is something amiss with someone who, say, finds no normatively motivating consideration in the fact that his mother needs help. The mental states are not *added*, in order to *explain* or *provide* the normative and motivational force of the reason; rather, they are simply identified third-personally as the *appropriate response* to the normative and motivational force of the reason.

A minor problem with this argument is that there appear to be two kinds of cases, running roughly along the lines of the permissible and the obligatory. There are cases in which the reason does seem to depend for its existence on a mental state, in particular a desire, and cases in which it does not. Suppose Jack's mother is not in need of help, and his only possible reason for going to Chicago would be that he would enjoy a visit with her. In that case, whether the fact that a trip to Chicago would procure his mother's company is a good-making property of going on the trip *does* depend on whether Jack desires to see his mother. And this may seem to suggest that some reasons do after all depend on mental attitudes and states. But this little difficulty may be finessed. The defender of the view that reasons are good-making properties may agree that one of the possible good-making properties of an action is that it that it satisfies the agent's desire – or perhaps more simply that it satisfies someone's desire.

But there is a deeper problem with the view that the mental states we sometimes mention when we are asked for our reasons are really just the appropriate responses to reasons that exist independently of them. For what does it mean to say that motivation or a sense of obligation is the *appropriate* response? That claim itself appears to be normative – we are not saying merely that it is the usual or natural response. So the idea seems to be that the mental states in question – desire or a sense of obligation or a belief in obligation or whatever it might be – are responses that there is reason to have. So now we seem to have reasons to be motivated and obligated by our reasons. The first layer of reasons are certain facts about the good-making properties of actions, and the second layer of reasons are facts about how it is appropriate to respond to those good-making properties. Do we then need a further layer of reasons about how it is appropriate to respond to the reasons in the second layer, and so on forever?

But the defender of good-making properties will again deny this. If someone fails to respond appropriately to the good-making properties of an action, one may argue, then he just is irrational, and that is all there is to it. That's what the normativity of the good-making properties of the action amounts to – that you are irrational if you don't respond to them in a certain way. In other words, rationality may simply be *defined* in terms of the appropriateness of certain responses. A practically rational being is *by definition* one who is motivated to perform actions by the perception or awareness of their good-making properties.[8]

But now we need to be more specific about what this means, for there are two possibilities here. One may perceive or be aware of X, but not under the description X. Does a rational agent find his reason in the good-making properties of the action themselves, or in the *fact* that those properties make the action good? Suppose it is good for a mother to protect her children from harm. Is a lioness who protects her cubs from a marauding male lion then acting for a reason, or rationally? Perhaps we do not know exactly how to think about the lionness's mental representations, but she is an agent, not a mechanism, and it seems clear that there is some sense in which she does what she does *in order to protect her cubs.*[9] That aim guides her movements, and in that sense motivates them; and given the risks to herself that she is prepared to run for the sake of her cubs, one may even be tempted to say that she acts under the influence of a normative claim. If this is all there is to rational agency, then of course it does not involve the exercise of any specifically human power which we might identify with the faculty of Reason: it is just a way we describe certain actions from outside, namely the ones that conform to rational principles or to the particular considerations we call "reasons."

On the other hand, we may insist that there *is* something different in the human case, something that does involve the faculty of Reason. The human being is aware of the reason *as a* reason; she identifies the good-making properties of the action under the description "good" or "reason" or "right," or some such normative description. She does not act merely in accordance with a normative consideration but *on* one. So rational action is not just a matter of being motivated by certain facts about the good-making properties of actions – say that the action will help one's mother, or that it would satisfy one's desire. Rather, it is a matter of being motivated by the awareness or belief that these facts *constitute* good-making properties of the action. To act rationally is to act from the belief that what you are doing is in some way good. But doesn't that show that the normative force belongs to a mental state after all?

To understand the answer, we must first ask what it means to believe that the facts constitute good-making properties. Recall that we are using 'good' here in a minimal and formal sense. To say that the facts constitute good-making properties in this sense is just to say that they provide the agent with what the agent regards as appropriate grounds for motivation. That's all goodness in this context is – appropriate grounds for motivation. So to say that you are motivated by the awareness that the good-making properties of the action make it good is just to say that you are motivated by the awareness that you have appropriate grounds for motivation. You are motivated by the idea that your motives are good. So rational motivation in a sense takes *itself* for its object. It has an essentially reflexive structure.[10] Kant at one point actually says something like this: he says we should act on maxims that can have as their objects *themselves* as universal laws of nature (G4:437; my emphasis).[11] It sounds very mysterious, and as if we had run into a problem, but I don't think that we have. I think this is just a way of saying that rational action is action that is *self-consciously* motivated, action whose motivation is essentially dependent on consciousness of its own appropriateness. It is this property – *consciousness of its own appropriateness* – that the lioness's motivation lacks.[12]

So to have a reason is to be motivated by the consciousness of the appropriateness of your own motivation. How is it possible to be in such a state? I will call this the problem of the reflexive structure of reasons. The problem is that you might think we have to choose between the two elements involved in the motivation. Either Jack is motivated by his mother's need for help, in which case one may complain that he is no more exercising reason than the lioness is; or Jack is motivated by the thought of his action's goodness, in which case one may complain that he is a self-absorbed jerk who really ought to be thinking about his mother instead of about how good his own actions are.

Aristotle and Kant, I am about to argue, show us the way around this: how the two elements of motivation, its content and the judgment of its goodness, may be combined. And this is no surprise, for to say that a rational agent is motivated by the appropriateness of being motivated in exactly that way is to articulate the deep root of Kant's dictum that a morally good agent acts not merely in accordance with duty but *from* it. In fact what I've just argued is that the problems usually associated with Kant's idea of acting from duty – the appearance that it somehow excludes acting from more attractive motives like a direct concern for others – is a problem that arises from the very nature of a reason for action. That is, once we understand that acting for a reason requires that one be conscious that one has a reason, we can also see that asking "Did he do it in order to help his friend, or because he thought it was his duty?" makes just as little sense as it would to ask, "Did he do it in order to help his mother, or because he thought he had a reason?" In order to explain how Aristotle and Kant solve the problem of the reflexive structure of reasons, I now to turn to the second of the three questions I raised: whether the reason for an action always rests in the goal that is achieved by it, or in other facts about the action.

IV. The Goodness of Action

According to a number of familiar theories of goodness, the standards of goodness for a thing are given by the nature of the thing itself, especially by its functional nature. A thing is good when it has the properties that make it good at being what it is, or doing what it does. If these theories are correct, then to determine what makes an action good, we ought first to ask what an action is – what its functional nature is – and then we will know what makes it good, to what standards it is subject.

Now John Stuart Mill thought he knew the answer to both of these questions. In the opening remarks of *Utilitarianism*, he says:

> All action is for the sake of some end, and rules of action, it seems natural to suppose, must take their whole character and color from the end to which they are subservient.[13]

According to Mill, action is essentially production, and therefore its function is to bring something about, to achieve some end. Whether an action is good, Mill concludes, depends on whether *what* it brings about is good, or as good as it can be.[14]

But it has not always seemed obvious to philosophers that action is essentially production. In Book VI of the *Nicomachean Ethics*, Aristotle says:

> Among the things that can be otherwise are included both things made and things done; making and acting are different.... so that the reasoned state of capacity to act is different from the reasoned state of capacity to make. Nor are they included one in the other, for neither is acting making nor is making acting. (NE VI.4 1140a1-15)[15]

According to Aristotle, action and production are two different things. And in the following section Aristotle remarks on one of the most important differences between them, namely that:

> while making has an end other than itself, action cannot; for good action itself is its end. (NE VI. 5 1140b5-10)

Actions, or at least good actions, Aristotle says, are chosen for their own sakes, not for the sake of something they produce.

Actually, this is one of three different things Aristotle tells us about why good actions are done by virtuous agents. First of all, in at least some cases an act is done for some specific purpose or end. For instance, Aristotle tells us that the courageous person who dies in battle lays down his life for the sake of his country or his friends (NE IX.8 1169a17-30). In the same way, it seems natural to say that the liberal person who makes a donation wants to help somebody out; the magnificent person who puts on a play wants to give the city a treat, the ready-witted man wants to amuse his audience, and so on. At the same time, as I've just mentioned, Aristotle says that virtuous actions are done for their own sakes. And finally, Aristotle also tells us that virtuous actions are done for the sake of the noble – *to kalon* (e.g. NE III.7 1115b12; III.8 1116b3; III.9 1117b9, 1117b17; III.11 1119b15; IV.1 1120a23; IV.2 1122b6).

If we suppose that the reason for an action rests in its purpose, as Mill does, these will look like three inconsistent or competing accounts of the purpose or aim of virtuous action. But when we consider Aristotle's own conception of an action we can see why there is no inconsistency here. What corresponds in Aristotle's theory to the description of an action is what he calls a *logos* – as I will render it, a principle. A good action is one that embodies the *orthos logos* or right principle – it is done at the right time, in the right way, to the right object, and – importantly for my purposes – with the right aim. To cite one of many such passages, Aristotle says:

> …anyone can get angry – that is easy – or give or spend money; but to do this at the right time, with the right aim, and in the right way, that is not for everyone, nor is it easy; that is why goodness is both rare and laudable and noble. (NE II.9 1109a25-30)

The key to understanding Aristotle's view is that the *aim* is included in the description of the action, and that it is the action as a whole, *including the aim*, which the agent chooses. Let us say that our agent is a citizen-soldier, who chooses to sacrifice his life for the sake of a victory for his polis or city. The Greeks seem to think that that is usually a good *aim*. Let's assume that our soldier also sacrifices himself at the right time – not before it is necessary, perhaps, or when something especially good may be achieved by it – say cutting off the enemy's access to reinforcements. And he does it in the right way, efficiently and unflinchingly, perhaps even with style, and so on. Then he has done something courageous, a good action. Why has he done it? His *purpose* or *aim* is to secure a victory for his city. But the object of his choice is the whole action – sacrificing his life in a certain way at a certain time in order to secure a victory for the city. He chooses this whole package, that is, to-do-this-act-for-the-sake-of-this-end – he chooses *that*, the whole package, as a thing worth doing for its own sake, and without any further end. "Noble" describes the kind of value that the whole package has, the value that he sees in it when he chooses it.

Now this means that Aristotle's view of the nature of action is the same as Kant's. Kant thinks that an action is described by a maxim, and the maxim of an action is also of the "to-do-this-act-for-the-sake-of-this-end" structure. Kant is not always careful in the way he himself formulates maxims, and that fact can obscure the present point, but on the best reading of the categorical imperative test, the maxim which it tests includes both the act done and the end for the sake of which that act is done. It *has* to include both, because the question raised by the categorical imperative test is whether there could be a universal policy of pursuing *this sort of* end by *these sorts of* means. For instance in Kant's own *Groundwork* examples the maxims tested are something like "I will commit suicide in order to avoid the personal troubles that I see ahead" and "I will make a false promise in order to get some ready cash." What the rejection of these maxims identifies as wrong is the whole package – committing suicide in order to avoid the personal troubles that you see ahead, and making a false promise in order to get some ready cash. The question of the rightness or wrongness of, say, committing suicide in order to save someone else's life, is left open, as a separate case to be tested separately. Indeed, Kant makes this clear himself, for in the *Metaphysics of Morals* he raises the question whether a man who has been bitten by a rabid dog and commits suicide in order to avoid harming others when he goes mad from the rabies has done something wrong or not.[16] Committing suicide in order to avoid seriously harming others is a different action from committing suicide in order to avoid the personal troubles that you see ahead, and requires a separate test.

And "moral worth" or being done "from duty" functions in Kant's theory in the same way that nobility does in Aristotle's. It is not an alternative purpose we have in our actions, but a characterization of a specific kind of value that a certain act performed for the sake of a certain end may have. When an agent finds that she *must* will a certain maxim as a universal law, she supposes that the action it describes has this kind of value. Many of the standard criticisms of the Kantian idea of acting from duty are based on confusion about this point.

The idea that acting from duty is something cold, impersonal, or even egoistic is based on the thought that the agent's *purpose* or *aim* is "in order to do my duty" *rather than* "in order to help my friend" or "in order to save my country" or whatever it might be. But that is just wrong. Sacrificing your life in order to save your country might be your duty in a certain case, but the duty will be to do that act *for that purpose*, and the whole action, both act and purpose, will be chosen as one's duty.

Let me introduce some terminology in order to express these ideas more clearly. Let's say that the basic form of a Kantian maxim is "I will do act-A in order to promote end-E." Call that entire formulation the description of an action. An action, then, involves both an act and an end, an act done for the sake of an end. In the examples we've been looking at, making a false promise and committing suicide are what I am calling "acts," or as I will sometimes say "act-types." Making a false promise in order to get some ready cash, committing suicide in order to avoid the personal troubles that you see ahead, and committing suicide in order to avoid harming others are what I am calling "actions."

Now a slight complication arises from the fact that *acts* in my sense are also sometimes done for their own sakes, for no *further* end, from some non-instrumental motive like anger or sympathy or the sheer pleasure of the thing.[17] In this case, doing the *act* is itself the end. To describe the whole *action*, in this kind of case, we have to put that fact into the maxim, and say that we are doing it for its own sake, for its inherent desirability, or however it might be. So for instance, if you choose to dance for the sheer joy of dancing, then *dancing* is the *act*, and *dancing for the sheer joy of dancing* is the *action*. We might contrast it to the different action of someone who dances in order to make money, or to dodge the bullets being shot at his feet. As I said before, it is the action that is strictly speaking the object of choice. And according to both Aristotle and Kant, it is the *action* that strictly speaking is, as Kant would have it, morally good, permissible, or bad; or as Aristotle would have it, noble, or at least not ignoble, or base.

The view that actions, acts-for-the-sake-of-ends, are both the objects of choice and the bearers of moral value sets Aristotle and Kant apart from many contemporary moral philosophers, less because of overt disagreement than because of unclarity about the issue. Here again, our ordinary practices of offering reasons give us unclear guidance. Earlier I noticed that when we ask for the reason for an action, we sometimes cite a fact, and sometimes a mental state.

But another way we often answer such questions, cutting across that debate, is to announce the agent's purpose. "Why did Jack go to Chicago?" "In order to visit his mother" is the reply. Jack's purpose is offered in answer to the question about his reason. This makes it appear as if his purpose is the reason for his choice, and as if what he chooses, in response to having that purpose, is only the act. But this appearance, I believe, is misleading.

To explicate this point I will first take a detour. One way to accommodate talk of reasons to the distinction I've just made between acts and actions would be to distinguish the reasons for acts from the reasons for actions. We could say that the act is performed for the sake of the purpose it serves, while the whole action is performed for its own sake – say because of its nobility or lawfulness or rightness. Then we might think that confusion arises from thinking there is always "a reason" for what someone does, when in fact the phrase "the reason for what he does" is ambiguous between the reason for the act and the reason for the action.

This proposal, although tempting, is not satisfactory. One problem with it springs from the fact that reasons are supposed to be normative. If a reason for an act is its purpose, and reasons are supposed to be normative, then it follows that the purpose itself is normative for the agent. This is certainly not what either Aristotle or Kant thinks. Kant does think that there are some purposes we ought to have – our own perfection and the happiness of others, which are identified as obligatory by his contradiction in the will test. These we must stand ready to promote if an opportunity comes in our way. But he does not think that our purposes are *in general* normative for us in this way. In Kant's theory, normativity arises from autonomy – we give laws to ourselves. But we do not first choose a purpose, enact it into law, and then scramble around for some way to fulfill it, now being under a requirement to do so.[18] If it worked that way, we *would* be in violation of a self-legislated requirement every time we gave up a purpose because we were unable to find a decent and reasonable way to achieve it. But this isn't what happens. If you can't get to Paris without stealing the ticket money, stowing away on a boat, or risking your life trying to cross the Atlantic in a canoe, then you may drop the project, and you have not thereby violated any norm.[19] What we will as laws are maxims, which describe actions, and we normally adopt a purpose as a *part* of an action.

Another problem with the proposal is that it suggests that in asking for "the reason" for what someone does, ordinary language is misleading, because there are always, so to speak, two reasons, one for the act and one for the action. But that in turn suggests a different way of looking at the situation, which does not require us to say that the idea of a reason is ambiguous, but only that we tend to misinterpret what we are doing when we offer a reason. If Aristotle and Kant are right about actions being done for their own sakes, then it seems as if every action is done for the same reason, namely because the agent thinks its worth doing for its own sake. This obviously isn't what we are asking for when we ask for the reason why someone did something, because the answer is always the same: he thought it was worth doing. What may be worth asking for is an *explication* of the action, a complete description of it, which will show us *why* he thought it was worth doing. Now normally we already know what the act was, so the missing piece of the description of the action is the purpose or end. "Going to Chicago in order to visit one's mother" is intelligible as a worthwhile thing to do, so once we have that missing piece in place, we understand what Jack did. That the purpose by itself couldn't really be the source of the reason shows up clearly in this fact: if the purpose supplied is one that fails to make the whole action seem worthwhile, even though the purpose is indeed successfully served by the act, we will not accept the answer. Suppose Jack lives in Indianapolis. Then if I tell you that Jack went to Chicago to buy a box of paperclips, you will not accept the answer, even though one can certainly buy a box of paperclips in Chicago. You will say "that can't be the reason," not because the purpose isn't served by the action, but because going from Indianapolis to Chicago just to buy a box of paperclips is so obviously not worthwhile. Thus when we ask for the reason we are not just asking what purpose was served by the act – we are asking for a purpose that makes sense of the whole action. And as Aristotle saw, there will be cases where supplying the purpose will not be sufficient to make the action intelligible even where it is, so to speak, weighty enough to support the act. "Why did Jack go to Paris?" we ask. "He has always wanted to see the Eiffel Tower" is the reply. "No, but why just now?" urges the questioner, for Jack has taken off quite suddenly in the middle of the semester. And as Aristotle says, in order to be worthwhile the action must also be done at the right time and in the right way. So the practice of answering the motivational question "why" by citing the agent's purpose does not really suggest that what we choose are acts, and our reasons are provided by our purposes. It is just that the purpose is often, though not always, the missing piece of the agent's maxim, the piece we need to have in place before we can see why the agent thought that this action as a whole was a thing worth doing.[20]

The way Kant presents the hypothetical and categorical imperatives in the *Groundwork* suggests that he himself may have fallen into the kind of confusion that I've been describing, at least about bad actions. He presents them as two different kinds of imperatives, on a footing with each other, and occasionally makes remarks suggesting that we are acting on either one *or* the other.[21] For instance at one point, after distinguishing the two imperatives, Kant contrasts someone who avoids making a false promise because it is "in itself evil" (G 4:419) with someone who avoids making a false promise because it will damage his reputation if it comes to light.

As I have already said, what Kant's view actually implies is "in itself evil" is making a false promise in order to get some money. But the slip is understandable, although this will take a moment to explain. As I mentioned before, on the best reading of the categorical imperative test, the question whether we can universalize the maxim is a question about whether we can will the universal practice of pursuing *that* end by *that* means. Or, to put the point more carefully, you ask whether you could will to be part of an order of things in which this was the universal practice, and at the same time rationally will the maxim in question yourself. For instance, you ask whether you could will to be part of an order of things in which everyone who needed money attempted to get it by means of a false promise, and at the same time will the maxim of getting money by means of a false promise yourself. According to Kant, in such an order of things people would just laugh at promises to repay money as vain pretences, rather than lending money on the strength of them (G 4:422). Since making a false promise would then not *be* a means of getting the money you need, you could not rationally will to get money by that means. And so the maxim fails the test.

This is not the place to discuss in detail how well this test works as a guide to moral judgment.[22] What I want to point out now is that there is one sort of case in which it works almost too well. Some act-types are purely natural, in the sense that they depend only on the laws of nature for their possibility. Walking and running, slugging and stabbing, tying up and killing – these are acts-types that are made possible by the laws of nature, and accordingly, one can do them in any society. Elsewhere I have noticed the difficulty of using the universal law test work to rule out maxims involving these kinds of acts.[23] But other act-types depend for their possibility not just on natural laws, but also on the existence of certain social practices or conventions. Writing a check, taking a course, running for office are act-types of this kind: you can only do them in societies with the sorts of institutions and practices that make them possible. Now where an action involves an act-type that must be sustained by practices and conventions, and at the same time violates those very practices or conventions, it is relatively easy to find the kind of contradiction that Kant looks for in the universalization test. This is because practices and conventions are unlikely to survive their universal abuse. Thus it hardly seems to matter *what* the purpose is for which you perform such an act; nearly every action involving such an act will fail the categorical imperative test. Charitably interpreted, Kant is recording this fact when he says that false promising is "in itself evil." Yet the remark is misleading at best. Even if Kant were right in thinking that any action involving the act-type "false promise" will fail the test, that wouldn't show that the act-type is inherently evil. It would only show that members of the class of actions involving that act-type are inherently evil.

No doubt remarks like the one about false promising being "in itself evil" are part of what has led to the widespread misconception that Kant's ethical system is supposed to generate rules against act-types. But this is not just a confusion about Kant's theory. It is a familiar confusion about ethics itself. And another thing that supports this confusion is the existence of words in the language that seem to name wrong act-types, but actually name wrong actions, though somewhat schematically described. Aristotle himself trips over this one when he says:

> But not every action nor every passion admits of a mean; for some have names that already imply badness... in the case of actions, adultery, theft, murder... nor does goodness or badness with regard to such things depend on committing adultery with the right woman, at the right time, and in the right way, but simply to do any of them is to go wrong. (NE II.6 1107a 9-15)

In fact, Aristotle is running together slightly different kinds of cases, but none of them shows that there are act-types that are inherently wrong. The example that best fits the point I want to make is murder. To say that murder is wrong is not to say that there is an act-type, murder, that is wrong no matter what end you have in view when you do it. Rather, "murder" is the name of a class of *actions*. A murder is a homicide committed for *some end or other* that is inadequate to justify the homicide. We don't call execution or killing in battle or killing in self-defense "murder" unless we believe that those actions are not justifiable, that punishment or war or self-defense are not ends that justify killing.

"Theft," another of Aristotle's examples, is not quite like that, or rather, it depends on how we are using the word. If by "theft" we mean "taking property that is not legally your own," we do have an act-type, but one that doesn't already imply wrongness, although it certainly gestures at a very likely reason for wrongness. It is like false promising – a violation of social practices that is *almost* sure to turn out wrong no matter what your end is. So here Aristotle may have been derailed by the same thing that derailed Kant. But of course there is a sort of colorful use of terms like 'theft' in which we do use them to indicate wrongness, precisely because the case *isn't* legally one of theft. Thus if a shop charges too much for an article people desperately need, we say "that's highway robbery!" to express our disapproval. In that usage, robbery or theft, like murder, already implies wrongness, but in that usage, theft is not an act-type. It is class of actions, roughly those that take people's property away for ends that can't justify doing that.

As for adultery, it also depends on the usage. If it means "having sexual relations with someone other than the person to whom you are married, or with a person who is married to someone else" it is like theft. It is an act-type, but again Aristotle is wrong. It *is* intelligible to ask whether perhaps at this time and in this place and with this particular person it is all right to commit adultery, just as it's intelligible to ask whether it is all right to violate society's property arrangements for some extraordinary purpose. Perhaps if your love is true and mutual and faithful, your spouse has been in a coma for the last fifteen years, the doctors say he is brain-dead but the law forbids removing life support, and divorce in these circumstances isn't legal, then adultery in this strictly legal sense isn't wrong – at least it makes sense to ask. But the word "adultery" may be used, like the word "murder," only to indicate *unjustifiable* violations of the marriage conventions. If one may say, without any misuse of language, "it isn't really adultery, for my husband and I have a very special understanding…" then "adultery" is like "murder", a term only used when we think the whole action is wrong.[24]

V. Motivation: the Relation Between Reasons and Actions

According to Aristotle and Kant, then, the object of choice is an action, in the technical sense I have explained – an act for the sake of an end. The reason for the action is expressed in the agent's *logos* or principle. Roughly speaking, what happens when an agent chooses an action is something like this: The agent is attracted on some occasion to promoting some end or other. The end may be suggested by the occasion, or it may be one he standardly promotes when he can. He reasons about how he might achieve this end, or what he might do in its service, and he arrives at a possible maxim or *logos*. He considers promoting a certain end by means of a certain act done in a certain way at a certain time and place. That is to say, he considers an action, and he asks himself whether it is a thing worth doing. And he determines the action to be noble or at least not base, morally worthy or at least permissible. Kant thinks he makes this determination by subjecting the maxim to a test, the categorical imperative test, and Aristotle does not, but for present purposes that is not important. Determining the action to be good, a thing worth doing for its own sake, he does the action. He is therefore motivated by the goodness of being motivated in the way he is motivated: or, to put it more intelligibly, by he is motivated by his awareness that his end is one that justifies his act in his circumstances, that the parts of his maxim are related in the right way.[25] Aristotle and Kant's view, therefore correctly identifies the kind of item that can serve as a reason for action: the maxim or *logos* of an action, which expresses the agent's endorsement of the appropriateness of doing a certain act for the sake of a certain end.

At the same time, their view brings out one of the ways in which having a reason is an exercise of an agent's activity. On their view, the agent chooses not only the act, but the purpose or end – he chooses the act for the sake of the end, but in doing so he chooses to promote or realize the end. Although his attraction to the end may be thrust upon him by nature, the decision to pursue the end is not. So choice on this view is a more fully active state than on the view that what we choose are mere acts, motivated by ends that are given to us. The agent does not just choose an act as a reaction to an end that is given him by his desire or even by his recognition of some external value. Since both the end and the means are chosen, the choice of an action is an exercise of the agent's own free activity.

But there is one last problem. Suppose someone objects that Aristotle and Kant's view does not actually solve the problem posed by the reflective structure of reasons. The Aristotelian or Kantian agent, the objector will say, is motivated by the nobility or moral worth of the whole action *rather than* by its content, by the end that it serves. I have still not shown that you can be motivated, as it were, in both ways at once. Nor (therefore) have I successfully shown that the agent is active in the way I've just claimed. On my theory of motivation, the agent's choice of the action is just a reaction to the goodness of the whole action, in the same way that, on the alternative theory, the choice of an act is just a reaction to the goodness of the end. So goes the objection.[26],[27]

This objection, I believe, is based on a fundamental misunderstanding of what it means to be motivated – a misunderstanding of the way in which reasons and actions are related. The objection assumes that a motivating reason is related to an action in the same way that a purpose is related to an act. The purpose is something separate from or outside of the act, for the sake of which one does the act. But the reason for an action is not related to an action in that way. So this brings us to the third question: how reasons and actions are related, or what it means to be motivated.

An essential feature of the view I have attributed to Aristotle and Kant is that the reason for an action is not something outside of or behind or separate from the action. Giving a description or explication of the action, and giving a description or explication of the reason, are the same thing. The *logos* or maxim which expresses the reason is a kind of description of the action, and could be cited in response to the question: *what is he doing?* just as easily as it can in response to the question *why is he doing that?* Indeed – to make one last appeal to our ordinary practices – their view explains why in ordinary language these questions are pretty much equivalent. For the demand for justification can as easily take the form: *what are you doing?* or more aggressively and skeptically *what do you think you are doing?* as it can *why are you doing that?* [28] The reason for an action is not something that stands behind it and makes you want to do it: it is the action itself, described in a way that makes it intelligible.

I can best convey what I have in mind here by drawing your attention briefly to the middle player in the trio of items that we associate with the idea of reason – principles. The agent's *logos* or maxim is, as Kant puts it, his subjective principle. What exactly is a principle, metaphysically speaking, and what does it mean to say that an agent has one or acts on one? Some recent moral philosophers have been critical of principles, thinking of them as something like rules that function as deliberative premises. "I believe in the principle of treating people equally, and therefore I will show these particular people no favoritism, though they happen to be my relatives." And then it may seem as if there is an option to acting on principle, such as being moved by love or compassion or loyalty instead.

But I don't believe that, at least for a rational agent, there is any option to acting on principle.[29] To believe in a principle is just to believe that it is appropriate or inappropriate to treat certain considerations as counting in favor of certain acts. Because that's what a principle is: a principle is a description of the mental act of *taking* certain considerations to count in favor of certain acts.[30] Suppose that Jack is tempted to take a trip to Chicago by the fact that it will help his mother, and he decides to act accordingly. The belief that the trip will help his mother does not cause him to act. Rather, he *takes* it to provide him with a reason for the action. We may represent this fact – his *taking* the fact that it would help his mother to count in favor of making the trip – by saying that it is his *principle,* his *logos* or maxim, to take a trip to Chicago in order to help his mother. So to say that he acts on principle is just to *record the fact* that he is active and not merely causally receptive with respect to his perception of the good-making properties of the action. Jack's actively, self-consciously, taking the fact that it will help his mother to count in favor of making the trip *amounts to* his judging that the whole action is good. And his taking the fact that it would help his mother as a reason for making the trip, and in so doing judging that the whole action is good, is coincident with his *doing it.*[31] I don't mean that he doesn't think, he just acts: as I said earlier, reasoned action is above all self-conscious. What I mean is that the judgment that the action is good is not a mental state that precedes the action and causes it. Rather, his judgment, his practical thinking, is embodied in the action itself. That's what it means to say that the action is motivated and not merely caused. For a motive is not merely a mental cause. And an action is not merely a set of physical movements that happens to have a mental cause, any more than an utterance is a set of noises that happen to have a mental cause. An action is an essentially intelligible object that *embodies* its reason, the way an utterance is an essentially intelligible object that embodies a thought. So being motivated by a reason is not a reaction to the judgment that a certain way of acting is good. It is more like an announcement that a certain way of acting is good. The person who acts for a reason, like God in the act of creation, *declares* that what he does is good.[32]

Notes

1. The answers admit of a rough, though only a rough, grouping. Empiricists tend to think that reasons are provided by our mental states, especially our desires; that the relevant facts con-

cern the desirability of the goals to be achieved through action; and that the relation between reasons and actions is causal. Rationalists tend to believe that reasons are provided by the facts in virtue of which the action is good, that these facts need not be limited to the desirability of the goals that are achieved through action, but may concern intrinsic properties of the action itself; and that the action is caused not by the reason, but rather by the agent's response to the reason. To some extent, this paper follows the familiar Kantian strategy of making a case by showing how the debate between rationalists and empiricists leads to an impasse.

2. These remarks are of course tautological; this is because the properties in question are essentially indefinable. These two properties I've just gestured at are sometimes referred to as normative and motivational internalism, respectively, but I prefer to avoid these terms.

3. Bernard Williams, *Ethics and the Limits of Philosophy* (Cambridge, MA: Harvard University Press, 1985), p. 19.

4. Joseph Raz, *Engaging Reason* (Oxford: Oxford University Press, 1999), p. 63. Raz actually says "options" not actions, but he means the actions among which we are choosing, so I've changed the quotation for clarity in this context.

5. In other words, I am looking for what it means to act for a reason in the descriptive sense of reason. An important feature of the terms "reason" "rational" and so forth is that they admit of either a descriptive or a normative use. In the descriptive sense, one can act "rationally" while acting for either a good reason or a bad one; rational action is opposed to non-rational action or perhaps mere movement or expression. In the normative sense, one counts as acting rationally only when the reason is good. Hence we can say either "that's a terrible reason" (descriptive sense) or "that's no reason at all" (normative sense) and mean the same thing. The point of focusing on the descriptive sense is that once we have identified which action or activity we have in mind when we talk about "acting for a reason," we may then be able to locate the normative sense by asking what counts as being *good at* this activity. As I will observe below, I think that the account of acting for a reason that I give in this paper supports the claim that acting in accordance with the categorical imperative is a way of being good at acting for a reason. See note 29.

6. St. Augustine, *Confessions* (trans. R. S. Pine-Coffin. Penguin Books, 1961), Book II. Section 4, p 47.

7. Elsewhere I have argued that this strategy cannot work, because it effectively blocks the attempt to give a descriptive account of what rationality is. See my "The Normativity of Instrumental Reason" in *Ethics and Practical Reason*, edited by Garrett Cullity and Berys Gaut (Oxford: Clarendon Press, 1997: pp. 213-254), p. 243. The argument of this paper is making good on that claim, even though in this paper I do not directly attack the idea of defining reason in terms of reasons.

8. For an argument that non-human animals count as agents see my *Self-Constitution: Agency, Identity, and Integrity*, forthcoming from Oxford University Press.

9. I can think of two other things that philosophers have claimed to have an essentially reflexive structure, or to take themselves for their objects. One is God, as conceived by Aristotle in *Metaphysics* XII.9, where God is identified with the divine activity of thinking on thinking – for Aristotle, the most perfect and purely active activity there can be. The other is personal identity. Some philosophers have claimed, rightly as I believe, that persons are not incidentally but essentially conscious of themselves. It's not as if you have a personal identity which you might or might not be conscious of; rather, if you are not conscious of your personal identity, then you don't have it. So the state of being a person takes itself for its object. [See for example Robert Nozick, *Philosophical Explanations* (Cambridge, MA.: Harvard University Press, 1981), Chapter I, Part II, pp. 71-114.] I am claiming reasons are like that, and in my

view this is no accident, since, as I argue in *Self-Constitution*, being a person is essentially an activity, and a person is in a sense constituted by her reasons.

10. References to Kant's *Groundwork of the Metaphysics of Morals* will be inserted into the text in the conventional fashion, using the volume and page numbers of *Kants gesammelte Schriften* (published by the Preussische Akademie der Wissenschaften, Berlin). Where I have quoted I have used the translation by Mary Gregor in the series Cambridge Texts in the History of Philosophy (Cambridge: Cambridge University Press, 1997).

11. Now at this point the defender of good-making properties may wish to argue as follows. The tangled formulation at which I have just arrived is result of the extremely broad definition of good-making property that I adopted at the outset. You will recall that I said that by good-making property I did not mean "good" in any substantial sense, but only whatever it is about the action that makes it seem eligible to the agent. If "eligible" means "appropriately motivating" then of course it follows that to be aware of the good-making properties is just to be aware of appropriate grounds for motivation. But the philosopher who proposes to define a rational agent as one who is moved by good-making properties does not mean good in this minimal or formal sense. Rather, the proposal here is that we define a rational agent as one moved by those properties that are genuinely good, in a substantial sense.

But this will not do. For we still have the problem of the lioness, and again she leaves us with two options. If protection of her cubs is genuinely good, in whatever substantial sense we have in mind, and to be rational is to be moved by the genuinely good, then on this showing she is a rational agent. Or if to avoid that, this philosopher accepts the claim that she must know her action is genuinely good, then all that this maneuver does is add an additional clause to my definition of rational agent. A rational agent is one who is motivated by the consciousness that her grounds for action are appropriate grounds for normative motivation *and gets it right*. This is not really a way of avoiding the issue.

What I have just said amounts to an argument to the effect that we must identify a descriptive sense of reason. See also notes 5 and 7.

12. John Stuart Mill, *Utilitarianism* (Indianapolis: Hackett Publishing, 1979), p. 2.

13. Actually, Mill is wrong about this. The theories of goodness I mention in the text seek to identify what are sometimes called "internal" or "constitutive" standards of goodness. These are standards that hold of an object in virtue of what it is. On Mill's own theory of action, the only constitutive standard of actions is effectiveness. The achievement of a good end, as opposed to whatever end is aimed at, is only an external standard for actions. Technically speaking, aiming at the good is a side constraint on action. For more on internal or constitutive standards see "The Normativity of Instrumental Reason" (cited above), especially pp. 249-250 and "Self-Constitution in the Ethics of Plato and Kant" (*The Journal of Ethics*, 3: 1-29, 1999: pp. 1-29), especially pp. 14-15.

14. References to Aristotle's *Nicomachean Ethics* will be inserted into the text, using the abbreviation NE followed by the book and section numbers, and then line and column numbers which refer to Immanuel Bekker's edition of the Greek text and which are standardly used in Aristotle scholarship. These numbers are found in the margins of nearly all translations. I have used the translation by W. D. Ross, revised by J. O. Urmson, which is found in *The Complete Works of Aristotle*, edited by Jonathan Barnes. Princeton: Princeton University Press: 1984.

15. Kant, *The Metaphysics of Morals*, trans. Mary Gregor. (Cambridge: Cambridge University Press, 1996), 6:423-424.

16. Kant's notorious example, from *Groundwork* I, of the sympathetic person who lacks moral worth, is like this: Kant specifies that he "has no further motive of vanity or self-interest" (G

4:398) and does the action for its own sake. The agent who acts from duty also does the action for its own sake. Discussions of the argument of *Groundwork* I frequently overlook this, and suppose instead that Kant is contrasting two different purposes one may have in one's actions, one's own pleasure and duty. For further discussion see my "From Duty and for the Sake of the Noble: Kant and Aristotle on Morally Good Action" (in *Aristotle, Kant, and the Stoics: Rethinking Happiness and Duty*, edited by Stephen Engstrom and Jennifer Whiting. New York: Cambridge University Press, 1996: pp. 203-236.), especially pp. 205-213. Kant does describe another of his *Groundwork* I exemplars, the prudent merchant, as performing an action for an instrumental reason (G 4:397). If the argument of this paper is correct, Kant should not have done that: the prudent merchant in fact chooses something like "to charge my customers a fair price in order to profit from the good reputation of my business" as an action worth doing for its own sake.

17. In the past I have sometimes suggested that Kant could be interpreted as allowing for maxims of having purposes – for instance in "Morality as Freedom" I imagine a maxim like this: "I will make it my end to have the things that I desire." [in *Creating the Kingdom of Ends* (New York: Cambridge University Press, 1996) p. 164) I now think that is wrong, and that purposes are adopted only as parts of whole actions, for reasons given in the text. The maxims associated with the contradiction in the will test should be understood as schematic maxims of action: roughly "I will do whatever I (decently and reasonably) can to promote the happiness of others and my own perfection."

18. I now think that what I say about this in "The Normativity of Instrumental Reason" (cited above) on pp. 245 ff., where I portray an agent as enacting ends into law prior to enacting means into law, is misleading. At the time I wrote that paper, I believed that its argument showed that hypothetical imperatives depended on categorical ones; I now believe it shows that, strictly speaking, there are no separate hypothetical imperatives. See note 20.

19. Gisela Striker reminds me that a word often translated from Greek as "reason" in the sense of "a reason" is *aition*, the why or the cause. The purpose of an action is its final cause, which appears as a part of the *logos*. Translations of this kind thus pick up the tendency to identify the reason with the purpose.

20. I have in mind remarks that suggest that bad or heteronomous action is done on hypothetical imperatives while good or autonomous action involves categorical imperatives. See for instance G 4:441, where Kant associates heteronomous accounts of morality with hypothetical imperatives. In fact, if actions are chosen for their own sakes, then every action is chosen in accordance with a law that has elements of both imperatives. The action must be chosen as something good in itself, which means it is governed by the categorical imperative. And every action must involve an act that is a means to an end, in a very broad sense of 'means' – it may cause the end, constitute it, realize it or whatever it might be. The right way to think of the law governing action, I now believe, is as a practical categorical imperative, where the instrumental element enters with the thought that the law must be practical.

21. For more extensive discussion see my "Kant's Formula of Universal Law" in *Creating the Kingdom of Ends* (New York: Cambridge University Press, 1996), pp. 77-105.

22. "Kant's Formula of Universal Law" (cited above), pp. 84-85 and 97-101.

23. It is a different question whether there are categories of actions that are always regrettable because they violate the (in this case, Kantian) ideal of human relationships – that there should be no coercion or deception. In "The Right to Lie: Kant on Dealing with Evil" (in *Creating the Kingdom of Ends*, cited above, pp. 133-158), I argue for a "double-level" interpretation of Kant's theory, with the Formula of Universal Law representing an absolute but minimal standard of justification, and the Formula of Humanity representing an ideal of human relations.

When dealing with evil agents or certain kinds of tragic circumstances, we may have to violate our ideal standards, but we are never justified in violating the Universal Law formula. The argument of this paper takes place in the terms of the Formula of Universal Law, and so is about what can be justified given the circumstances, not about the ideal. I thank Marian Brady for pressing this question, and Tamar Schapiro for discussion of the issue.

24. Elsewhere I have argued that Kant's notion of the form of a maxim can be understood in terms of Aristotle's sense of "form." A thing's form in Aristotle's sense is the arrangement of its parts that enables it to perform its function. In a good maxim, the act and the end are related to each other in such a way that it can serve as a universal law. [see Korsgaard, *The Sources of Normativity* (Cambridge: Cambridge University Press, 1996), §3.3.5, pp. 107-108]. I have also suggested that we might understand Aristotle's notion of the *orthos logos* in the same way – the parts are all related in a way that gives the action its nobility. See "From Duty and for the Sake of the Noble: Kant and Aristotle on Morally Good Action" (cited above), p. 218.

25. Notice that if this objection were correct, merely permissible action would not be possible, or at least there would be a difficulty about it, since in that case the action is judged to be "not bad" or "not ignoble" and that hardly sounds like a reason for doing it. The content of the maxim must play a role in motivation if permissible action is possible. The account I am about to give shows how permissible action is compatible with autonomy.

26. Another way to put the objection, or at least a similar objection, is to wonder why "doing my duty" should not be regarded as a further end, to which the action as a whole serves as a kind of means. In this case the answer is to start the argument over, and to ask whether it is the fact that the action is a means to doing one's duty, or the agent's belief that the action is a means to doing his duty, that serves as the reason for doing it. We can only solve the problem by supposing that reasons have a reflexive structure, and to explain how that is possible, we have to come around once more to a view like Aristotle and Kant's – understood as I have presented it in the text.

27. Despite the apparent complexity of their view, the idea behind Aristotle's and Kant's conception of what it means to have a reason is in one way simpler than that of their contemporary competitors. To have a reason is to be motivated by certain considerations, taking them to be appropriate grounds for motivation. To have a reason, in other words, is *to know what you are doing*.

28. Actually, I believe that there is also a sense in which non-human animals act on principle: their instincts serve as their principles. See my "Motivation, Metaphysics, and the Value of the Self: A Reply to Ginsborg, Schneewind, and Guyer" [*Ethics* 109 (October 1998): pp. 49-66], especially pp. 49-51, and my forthcoming book *Self-Constitution: Agency, Identity, and Integrity* (cited above, note 8).

29. The categorical imperative, in its universal law formulation, is in a way both descriptive of and normative for this act. It is descriptive insofar as the agent who takes end-E to count in favor of doing Act-A in effect makes "doing Act-A for the sake of End-E" her law, the law that governs her own action. It is normative insofar as it indicates what counts as performing this act well – namely, reflecting on whether that maxim is really fit to serve as a law. See note 5.

30. It is frequently argued that intentions must exist separately from actions because we often decide what we will do (and why) in advance of the time of action. I believe, however, that we begin implementing or enacting our decisions immediately, for once a decision is made, our movements must be planned so that it is possible to enact it. I thank Luca Ferrero for illuminating discussions of this issue.

31. I would like to thank Charlotte Brown, Tamar Schapiro, Ana Marta González, for valuable comments on drafts of this paper. I would also like to thank audiences at the Catholic Univer-

sity of America, the University Carlos III in Madrid, the University of Navarra, the University of Virginia, and the University of Illinois at Urbana-Champaign for helpful discussion. The arguments of section IV are drawn from my 2002 Locke Lectures (forthcoming as *Self-Constitution: Agency, Identity, and Integrity*, cited above) and in that form were presented to an audience at Oxford, whom I also thank for discussion.

Danish Yearbook of Philosophy, Vol. 40 (2005), 37-56

THE NECESSITY OF POLITICS

DICK HOWARD

SUNY at Stony Brook

Since the Fall of the Berlin Wall in 1989, political philosophy has been adrift, the well- worked opposition of deontological liberalism and attempts to (somehow) update the Marxist philosophy of praxis have lost their utility for either understanding or changing the world. But it's hard to give up the old certitudes and set out for new horizons. As a compromise, attempts have been made to adapt the old orientations and language to the new world. The result appears as a new opposition between the quest to realize a system of international law and the attempt to invent a new form of cosmopolitanism. Some might see these two approaches as the contemporary version of the old opposition, the former representing a creative adaptation of the liberal paradigm while the latter – building on the insights learned from the development of an autonomous civil society in East Central Europe that was crucial to the liberation of 1989 – takes the form of a new cosmopolitanism. It seems to me, however, that the two share a common set of presuppositions. They begin from the notion that the end of communism means that we now live in One Global World which, however, exists only *an sich* until a politics can be invented that will help it to become *für sich*. The partisans of a new cosmopolitanism claim that they hold the needed conceptual orientation, while the defenders (and critics) of a new international legal framework propose their own variant. The problem in both cases, however, is that this manner of formulating the challenge of our new age is essentially *anti-political*. The quest for unity leaves no place for difference, the demand for universality occludes the place of the particular, and practice becomes the agent of theory.

Rather than remain within the old signposts, I want to propose here a different conceptual framework. My starting point is the events of 1989 and their interpretation. These events mark the end of what I call "two hundred years of error" by returning to the political agenda the need to develop an understanding of democracy as itself a radical force.[1] My suggestion is that democracy emerged onto the agenda of Western societies with the American and then with the French revolutions. But in their wake, political philosophy did its level best to tame the new force. The tools available, or invented, for this project included from the liberal perspective the juridification of social relations, their subsumption under imperatives of bureaucratic or technocratic logic, or (perhaps?) the pragmatic turn denounced by the Frankfurt school's Max Horkheimer, in *The Eclipse of Reason*, for its abandonment of any critical perspective. From the side of the philosophers of praxis, the appeal to an economic infrastructure and the necessity of an historical transformation incarnated in the proletariat that would put, finally, and end to class struggle, served a similar function. In both cases, *politics (and political theory) became anti-political.*

In order to recapture the political potentiality that was (re-)opened by the unexpected breakdown of the old order in 1989, it is necessary first to get a clear sense of what is meant by *anti-politics*. I will try to give the reader an intuitive sense of what is meant by this concept by first of all explaining the title of this essay: what is meant by "the necessity of politics"? That will clear the way for a more conceptual approach, which is developed by taking seriously Marx's work – all of it! – as philosophy, indeed as *systematic philosophy*[2]. While Marx described with brio and brilliance the emergence of democratic society, it was just this systematic imperative that led him to misunderstand his own achievement. But democracy is not a "thing" that can be described by the outside spectator; it represents a particular kind of social relations that emerges, when there exists no external constraint that weighs upon the free creation of social relations of autonomy. As a result, democracy is not achieved, once and for all; it is constantly challenged by its own premises, which is why it cannot be reduced to any simple institutional structure. If we return to the two paradigm cases of a democratic revolution, we find that each of them went through a series of developments marked by an attempt to put an end to the disquieting experience on which they had embarked. Each sought stability and unity through recourse to a constitution embodying the universalist principles of the enlightenment. In each of them we encounter the temptation to anti-political methods.

The difference between the two foundational democratic revolutions can be summed up by the opposition between a "republican democracy" and a "democratic republic." The latter orientation, typified by the French revolution, seeks to use the power of the state in order to transform society in such a way as to overcome the tension between the universality of the state and the particularity of society. The former political form emerged gradually in the new United States as their experiment was driven forward by its own inner logic, and by the force of external events. While the bases of the republican democracy were formulated implicitly in the new constitution of 1787 (that replaced the earlier Articles of Confederation), it was not until the new institutions were faced with a challenge that had not been expected – the emergence of a competitive system of opposed political parties – that their full implications could become apparent. And even then, the new democratic politics that emerged was short-lived, disappearing and reappearing in the course of an American history that has still not come to an end.

Although I suggest that democracy represents a new vision of politics that could find its place in our twenty-first century world, it is necessary to add that it is not a "solution" to the questions that have always haunted political thought and action. Indeed, as we've known since Athens, democracy stands also as a threat to itself and there is no way that this danger can be avoided once and for all. The question is then: how can we live with the challenges posed by this modern type of social relations? In the concluding sections of this paper, I try to suggest the need to pass from a "politics of will" to a "politics of judgement." The former corresponds to the type of politics inaugurated by the quest for a democratic republic in the French revolution, while the latter finds its practical foundation in the experience of its American cousin. Once again, the two orientations are not water-tight but can always bleed into the other as conditions change and actors lose touch with the historical and theoretical basis of their respective systems. That is why I've titled this paper as I have.

1. The Necessity of Politics

My title could also be read as an allusion to Marx's 11th *Thesis on Feuerbach*, whose imperative formulation reminds us that philosopher's have only interpreted the world, whereas the point is to change it. But that is not what I intend to argue; and I will devote part of this discussion to showing why Marx misunderstood both the nature (and limits) of philosophy and that of politics. But there are errors that are fruitful, as long as their origin and their immanent logic are made clear. Marx has to be criticized, but he has also to be taken seriously. A year or so after he wrote the *Theses on Feuerbach*, Marx sat down in Brussels and penned another famous aphorism: "A specter is haunting Europe, the specter of Communism." What he described in *The Communist Manifesto* was in fact the birth of democracy, but he didn't know it. The democracy he described was not, of course, what political scientists understand by the term – an institutional structure with elections, competing political parties, policy debates and the like. Marx always remained, *malgré lui*, a philosopher. What he described was the birth of a democratic *regime*, a type of social relations whose uniqueness I will try to illustrate in a moment[3]. To do that, however, it is necessary first to ask why Marx, and then later Marxists, did not understand what he was in fact describing?

Why did Marx not understand politics? Or, alternatively, what did he think was the nature of politics? The question suggests a further implication of my title. Marx thought of true politics as *revolutionary*. He assumed that not just everyday political activity but also the sudden upheavals that he described in essays like *Class Struggles in France* or *The Eighteenth Brumaire* could be understood, in the last instance, as the result either of underlying socio-economic conditions, or the misguided, ideological self-understanding of actors unable to face the demands of the true revolution that was on History's agenda. That historical Agenda was what Marx thought had been revealed by *The Communist Manifesto* which, as its title suggests, claims to make manifest an underlying truth that is brought from the darkness into the light. In this sense, Marx's theory belongs to one strand of the Enlightenment. But the politics of revolution does not fit so well with the goals of that movement – despite the attacks of its enemies who seek to blame the *philosophes* for the excesses of the French revolution, and even for the revolution itself, and despite the claims of some of its Marxist friends for whom the progression from 1789 to 1793 was completed only in 1917. Once again, the error that permits Marx to make his strong case for politics as revolution will prove fruitful by making it necessary to distinguish a (revolutionary) politics of will from a (democratic) politics of judgement.

There is one other fruitful misinterpretation of the enlightenment legacy that has roots in Marx. This one identifies politics with demystification, either of forms of false consciousness or of the relations of power that are masked by such ideologies. It is one thing to denounce the injustices of our societies and to wish to *écraser l'infâme*. The reader of *Capital* is literally swamped with information about its ill-effects – think, for example, of the long chapter on the working day in volume I. But that's not all that is intended by the author of *Das Kapital* – which is given that title, rather than the future-oriented etiquette of, say, "Communism," because its analysis presents not just a polemical *criticism* but rather an *immanent critique*. The goal of such critique, which explains Marx's title, was expressed already by the young Marx when he demanded that we "make those petrified relations dance by singing before them their own melody" (diese versteinerten Verhältnisse zum tanzen zwingen, indem wir ihnen ihre eigene Melodie vorsingen). Within the appearing relations of modern society, Marx implied, lie the normative seeds of a better, more rational and therefore more just society. Immanent critique separates the goals of the Enlightenment from utopian projects; but its attachment to an implicit philosophy of history limits its reach to modern social relations. It calls for a kind of phenomenological approach to political history that I have tried to put into practice in *Aux origines de la pensée politique américaine*.[4]

A final point needs to be mentioned with regard to my title. The pre-exile Frankfurt School understood the idea of immanent critique as the positive lesson to be inherited from philosophical enlightenment – for example, in the two essays of 1936-37 in which Horkheimer and Marcuse explain the nature of their Critical Theory. But the secret foundation of their hopes was a Marxist vision of history; and their experience of two totalitarianisms along with American exile led Horkheimer to a more undifferentiated evaluation of the historical record, developed a century after Marx's *Manifesto*, when he and Adorno wrote the *Dialectic of Enlightenment*. In their dark vision, the paradoxical result of the historical process of enlightenment that for them now began with the Greeks has become a totally administered world populated by subjects who have lost their subjectivity. The post-modernist relativism that transforms their analysis into a cheery optimism that rejoices in the discovery of ever-new "resistances" (in the plural) is no more capable of rediscovering the virtues of the politics of immanent critique than is the dour practice of denunciation that expends its positive energy in the discovery that the global glass is always half empty. Each of these orientations is unsatisfactory on its own; and each of them can lay claim to some aspect of Marx's legacy and its links to the Enlightenment. This warrants a closer look at Marx himself. What is his error, and why is it fruitful? And what does it tell us about politics?

2. Systematic Philosophy: the Source of Fruitful Errors

I've tried to show elsewhere that there is a unity in Marx's work; and that unity is defined by his systematic philosophical project. The earliest formulation of this project is found in a note added to Marx's doctoral dissertation, to which his editors gave the title: On the becoming philosophical of the world as the becoming worldly of Philosophy. (Philosophisch-werden der Welt als weltlich-werden der Philosophie.) Marx's philosophical-political intuition was that one must show *both* that philosophy *must* become worldly and the world *must* become philosophical. This double imperative must be realized at one and the same time, in one and the same movement, and with a necessity that is systematic. In the twin essays of 1843, "On the Jewish Question" and then the "Introduction to a Critique of Hegel's *Philosophy of Right*," this imperative already gives rise to typical two-sided formulae, such as the weapon of critique is the critique of the weapons or the demonstration that the "practical party" cannot succeed without the "theoretical party" and vice-versa. The demonstration then culminates in the discovery of the revolutionary proletariat as the subject-object of history: it is the product of past history that is capable (for historical reasons) of seizing hold of that history and inventing a new one. All that is needed for the hour of emancipation is that the "lightning of thought" strike this "naïve soil of the people." But that metaphoric lightning could not yet satisfy Marx's philosophical quest for systemic completeness.

The double imperative of Marx's philosophy can be understood as the attempt to unite a phenomenological (or genetic) account with a logical (or normative) analysis in order to produce a systematic dialectic. Thus, in the *1844 Manuscripts*, a first phenomenological essay denounces alienated labor but breaks off, seemingly unable to see how the dilemma it discovers can be overcome; a new essay then moves forward in terms of a logical clash between capital and labor, at first working together for the shared good, then recognizing their own proper interest, before a final clash must occur. The third manuscript, famous for its vision of "the greatness of Hegel's *Phenomenology*" seeks a synthesis in the notion of labor. When this too is finally not produced, Marx leaves behind the attempt at critical appropriation of philosophy to work toward a new systematic vision in the historical materialism of *The German Ideology*.

But philosophy, with its double, systematic imperative continues to be present in the later works. Perhaps the best illustration is found in a long argument in the *Grundrisse*.[5] To be complete, the account of the necessary dissolution of capitalism must have four distinct moments corresponding to the genetic and the normative expressions of use value and exchange value. From the side of capital, the demonstration must show (1) that it develops use-values whose realization is blocked by its one-sided stress on exchange value; and (2) that even on its own terms it produces economic crises caused by the pressure of competition that drives it beyond its own limits. This dual contradiction must be accompanied on the side of labor by the demonstration (3) that "civilizing" processes occur within the alienation of capitalist production that produce a new "wealth" of needs and capacities which form the basis of a new form of social relations; and (4) that the labor theory of value is made obsolete by economic development itself such that alienated labor can no longer reproduce capitalist social relations. Enough has been said about the economic problems in capitalism's self-realization; while it will not break down on its own, the crises that plague its process of reproduction cannot be denied. The other three moments are developed in a brief but lucid – even prophetic – account of fully realized capitalism at the beginning of Notebook VII of the *Grundrisse*. While its arguments explain Marx's expectation in the *Critique of the Gotha Program* that, in the second phase of communism, "the springs of wealth" will flow freely, they also suggest the need to reconstruct a normative notion of the political that can replace capitalism's "obliteration" of that domain.

Marx argues that the complete development of capital takes the form of modern industry based on machinery. In these conditions, it is not the "direct skillfulness" of the worker but "the technological application of science" that is the crucial productive force. (Gr, 699) At first, this appears to produce a "monstrous disproportion between the labor time applied and [the value of] its product..." (Gr, 705) And "the human being comes to relate more as watchman and regulator of the production process itself," inserting "the process of nature, transformed into an industrial process, as a means between himself and inorganic nature, mastering it." (Id) From the standpoint of exchange value, the worker simply stands at the side of the process; he is present "by virtue of his presence as a social body." But *this is where the process inverts itself*. "It is, in a word, the development of the social individual which appears as the great foundation-stone of production and of wealth." And, Marx continues, *"the theft of alien labor time on which present wealth is based is a miserable foundation in the face of this new one"* (Id, Marx's emphasis). This account goes beyond the abstract individualist view of alienated labor formulated in 1844. Its economic premises have systematic philosophical consequences.

Beginning from the side of labor (4) the development of productivity by the application of science that makes nature work for man means that labor time ceases to be the measure of value. Production based on exchange-value breaks down of its own accord. The growth of the power of social production increases the disposable time available to society, which at first falls to the capitalists and their class. But as this disposable time grows, it becomes clear that "real wealth is the developed productive power of all individuals. *The measure of wealth is then not any longer, in any way, labor time, but rather disposable time."* (Gr, 708, my stress) Capitalism contains a "moving contradiction" which leads it to reduce labor time to a minimum even while postulating labor time as the measure and source of wealth. Further, (3) since work has become supervisory and regulatory, the worker recognizes that "the product ceases to be the product of isolated direct labor; rather it is the combination of social activity that appears as the producer." (Gr, 709) Individual labor has now become social labor – not as producing exchange value but use-value. In addition, "[f]ree time – which is both idle time and time for higher activity – has naturally transformed its possessor into a different subject, and he then enters into the direct production process as this different subject." (Gr, 712) But (2) capital seeks to limit the new human possibilities in accord with its own concept of wealth. If it succeeds, this will lead to surplus production that cannot be sold, and necessary labor will be interrupted because the surplus labor already produced cannot be realized as capital. Finally (1) its normative orientation to exchange value may slow the development of new productive techniques because it refuses to admit that the priority of "[t]he free development of individualities, and hence not the reduction of necessary labor time so as to posit surplus labor, but rather the general reduction of the necessary labor of society to a minimum, which then corresponds to the artistic, scientific etc. development of the individuals in the time set free, and with the means created, for all of them." (Gr, 706) The four moments necessary to the transcendence of capitalism *on its own basis* are now present.

The demonstration is magnificent in its systematic rigor; but it tells us nothing about politics, and nothing at all about the democracy that – I claimed at the outset of this discussion – was what Marx was in fact describing. Marx seems to give too much weight to philosophy and its rational imperatives, and too little to the particularity of politics. If we continue to look at Marx to try to find the fruitful errors from which we can still learn, we have to take at face value Marx's claim – presented in the *Jewish Question* and present throughout his writing, that "merely formal democracy" is insufficient. Such a democracy expresses a form of alienation that needs to be overcome. Just as philosophy must become worldly as the world becomes philosophical, so too democracy must become worldly as the world becomes democratic. This would be the task of the Marx's revolutionary politics, which is inscribed in the historical existence of capitalism whose secret *telos* he claimed to have made manifest in his famous pamphlet. We need to look more closely at this idea of politics as revolution – or revolution as politics. The continued stress on systematic imperatives in Marx suggests that philosophy tends to replace politics – in spite of the claim of the 11th *Feuerbach Thesis*.

3. Democratic Republic or Republican Democracy?

I have argued elsewhere that the French revolution gave birth to the quest for a "democratic republic" whereas its American cousin produced a "republican democracy". There is no need to stress that the French version was quite theoretically self-conscious – to the point that it seems often that it was the rigor of its own theoretical quest that prevented it from finding a means to put a stop to its onward rush. Hegel understood well the stakes, and sought to avoid the radical outcome, by treating the *will* as the principle of his *Philosophy of Right*. And Habermas, developing arguments implicit in Marx, showed nearly 40 years ago that Hegel's account made revolution into the principle of philosophy, which was thereby de-fanged. The argument, however, rings true to both text and context; but the conclusion follows only if the theory of history as leading to the overcoming of all antagonisms is accepted – only if history will conclude, as with Marx's *Grundrisse*, in a grand Aufhebung, and politics is therefore to be understood as identical to revolution. The American experience, and its results, suggest a different – a democratic – interpretation of politics. From the "self-evident" truths proposed by the Declaration of Independence to the attempt to put them into practice once independence was insured, the idea of a unique popular will incarnate in political decisions was challenged. The new constitution elaborated in 1787, and especially the first years that tested and tempered its institutions presented a different vision of the political sphere, what I call a politics of judgement.

The crucial distinction between the two republican visions is that the democratic republic seeks an adequation (or more strongly: an identification) of the *demos* that has conquered its sovereignty with the government that is to be its representative. One sees here why Marx falls to this side of the division. Francois Furet, precisely because of his self-critical reflection on his communist past, understood well the logic of the situation. His well-titled, reflective volume of 1978, *Penser la révolution française*, refused to simplify the analysis by preaching to the converted (what he called the "edifying" discourse of identity); instead, he chose to follow a critique of the orthodox interpretation with a lucid and sympathetic presentation of two completely opposed visions of the

revolution, that of Alexis de Tocqueville, for whom it is the result of a long
term process and for whom it begins really already in 1787, and that of Au-
gustin Cochin, who traces the development of the enlightenment sociétés de
pensée which created a kind of actor who was no longer bound by the limits of
the old hierarchies. One sees here why the philosophical Marx would have
been attracted to such a vision: it joins together the genetic (activist) short-
term perspective with the normative (historical) vision of a deeper seated evolution. But the fate of that philosophical politics was ultimate failure: the temporary liberal (or "English") constitutional synthesis had to be unstable;
Girondins had to be overthrown by the Jacobins, and the triumph of Robe-
spierre as the incarnate voice of the people was in turn fated to disappear because it appeared to freeze and fix the revolution in a single personage (as
Baczko shows nicely in *Sortir de Thermidor*). Inadequate as practical politics,
the philosophical synthesis provides an interpretive framework that permits
understanding the root of that failure. Philosophy cannot *be* politics, but it can
help to understand politics. Politics remains necessary.

   With the transformation of the revolution into Napoleon's empire, and the
subsequent series of failed revolutions during the French 19th century, it
seemed that revolutionary politics remained on the agenda. 1793 remained "
une date charnière," and for many its consummation was 1917. But 1917 has
come and by 1989 it had gone. In fact, the politics of revolution had lost its appeal long before then. The new critical understanding challenged the totalitarian result of the quest for the realization of a democratic republic; but it did not
fall back on the globalized philosophical vision of the *Dialectic of Enlightenment*. It took seriously instead another aspect of the Enlightenment, the so-
called liberal idea of the rights of man. Its goal was the creation of a civil society based on a solidarity that did not need to conquer the summits of state power in order to use it to transform society. The basis of this new development
was the recognition that *if it were realized, a democratic republic would leave
no room for politics*. If the sovereign will were able to externalize itself, to represent itself truly and fully, there would be neither space nor time for political
judgement and rational discourse. This is implicit in Rousseau's distinction of
the volonté générale from the volonté de tous, since the former – which points
toward the ideal of the democratic republic – exists or doesn't exist, and leaves
no room for deliberation. The politics of revolution as realized in the democratic republic are in fact an *anti-politics*. When framed in that context, it is possible to understand how *the rights of man are a politics* and not simply a set of

moral imperatives. But "that context" – the framework of the democratic republic" – does not exist always and everywhere. The rights of man need not always be a politics, as I'll try to suggest when I return to our contemporary problem of cosmopolitanism and the crisis of international law. For the moment, it is necessary to complete this historical-philosophical discussion by turning to the American revolution, whose perhaps most famous founding document, the Declaration of Independence, is usually read as the proclamation of a natural law-based theory of rights – despite its appeal to "a candid world" for the political support that the Americans knew realistically to be necessary.

To understand how the Americans came to create a republican democracy, it is necessary to recognize that their revolution continued over a period of at least 40 years (from 1761 through 1803); indeed, in one sense, the republican democracy creates the conditions for a kind of permanent revolution. The "date charnière" that has to be understood is 1800. It signals the vicious political campaign (like that of 2004) which saw the first real opposition between different political orientations. While the Marxist might try to reduce these to the material interests that they represented, that would be a diversion from the real question. After all, Jefferson stood for a vision of a rural economy (with slave labor) while Adams's northeastern constituents were more urban and industrial. But the real question is not why Jefferson won, but why did the partisans of Adams leave office so peacefully. After all, the peaceful passage of power from one party to another was a political innovation that had not happened before, anywhere or anytime in history. The answer, I've tried to show elsewhere, is contained in the long history by which the revolution came gradually to recognize its own political nature[6]. This process was not so simple as the usual portrait that opposes a purely political revolution to a movement that goes beyond the merely political to attempt a social transformation – presented famously by Hannah Arendt in *On Revolution*, but invented in fact by Friedrich Gentz, the disciple of Burke who would later be Metternich's secretary at the Congress of Vienna, whose pamphlet proposing this interpretation was translated into American by John Quincy Adams as a way of supporting his father's campaign against the Francophile Jefferson.

The American colonists did not seek to make a revolution; like many colonies before and since then, these outsiders were overly loyal and desirous to imitate their masters. But once the British had driven their French rivals from the continent at the end of the Seven Years' War, the colonists felt no more need of protection at a time when the British were attempting to pay the costs of the war by the attempt to reorganize (and finance) the administration of their newly won empire. Between 1761 and 1776, a battle of pamphleteers took place, punctuated by political events that had to be taken into account as the arguments spiraled toward their culmination in the Declaration of Independence. At issue throughout this period was the question of *sovereignty* (and its practical implication, the right to lay taxes). Without going into the details of the effort at practical political philosophy undertaken, some moments of its practice that were vital to the developing opinions should be noted. When the British proposed a Stamp Tax, the Americans replied by non-compliance, learning in the process that they had no need of the symbols of British authority to conduct their daily affairs. In reply to other taxes, movements of non-importation were organized – and enforced by local patriots – with the implication that the self-government of the colonies was possible. And, of course, there was the Boston Tea Party. But mostly, there were pamphlets, arguments and debates in a literate society used to its autonomy.

The Declaration of Independence that was the upshot of these years of practical polemic is usually cited for its affirmation of "self-evident rights" that appeal to the judgement of "a candid world." But the Declaration is not reducible to a Lockean theory of natural law; the major part of its text consists in demonstrating that the British have undertaken a long-term plot to suborn American autonomy. This suggests that the issue of political sovereignty, not that of private rights, was primary for the Americans. Such a concentration on a plot to snuff out their liberties is a reflection of an "Old Whig" orientation to politics. It reflects the idea that power always seeks to expand its domain at the expense of liberty. It does so by what is called "corruption," by which is meant the appeal to the vanity, the egoism and self-seeking of the people. That is why the Declaration argues that "we" have warned our British brethren, who have remained deaf to our appeal; and that it is necessary that we separate from them before it is too late. (The Declaration is in this sense the reflection of an elite acting for the good of the nation.)

The military victory achieved finally in 1781 (with French help) prepared the politics of the next stage. If independence was necessary in order to assure the sovereignty that was threatened by the corruption used by Great Britain to enslave its colonies, it would seem that the newly independent colonies would be able to make their way as a self-created democracy. But the constitution of the entity that had fought the British and been supported by the French (and the Dutch) was that of a Confederation. There was no national power, even at the most crucial phases of the war of independence. And once that battle was won, there seemed to be no need to create a new central authority. The Articles of Confederation gave each state its head, while the nation as a whole went through a depression at the end of the war. Of all the states, the most radical was Pennsylvania, where for historical reasons, the elite that, elsewhere, had rallied to the cause of independence, supported the monarch. Pennsylvania's constitution was that of a radical democracy, one that some commentators have compared to that of the Jacobins in 1793. In its practice, with yearly elections, constant public intervention, regular revision of laws, its results were economic uncertainty and political unease. Pennsylvania's experience served as a kind of negative model for the elite who gathered in 1787 in Philadelphia (the largest city in the union) to propse a new constitution to the nation. Its experience showed that the sovereignty of the people could not be directly exercised, that the popular passions needed to be at once expressed and controlled, and that a new constitution would have to face up to that task.

The question of sovereignty remained present in the constitutional assembly, and even more so in the debates that led to the ratification. The philosophical question that underlay these arguments can be summed up by comparing three of the essays, published in popular newspapers under the name of "Publius," by John Jay, James Madison, and Alexander Hamilton. Collected under the name *The Federalist*, the 10th essay returns to the question of sovereignty and the dangers of a direct democracy[7]. The *Federalist*'s argument goes back to the history of political philosophy, which had worried always about problems of faction. Its claim is that just because of the great extent of the American republic – which localists had used as an argument against the new constituition – the danger of faction will be reduced while the room needed for freedom is preserved. The extended republic would suffice to avoid the threat of despotism. But then, somewhat later, in Federalists 48-51, and particularly in 51, one finds the argument that the danger of faction will be avoided not because sovereignty is divided but because of the institutional division of powers – which does not consecrate an Aristotelian-Polybian mixed sovereignty but rather uses the institutions of government to provide not just a division of powers but *checks and balances*.

This resolution of the problem of sovereignty is either too powerful or self-contradictory. Either Federalist 10 suffices; we then have a material solution in the extended republic. Or Federalist 51 suffices, and we have now an institutional solution. The difficulty emerges fully only in Federalist 63, which asks why there should be a Senate. After all, the political tradition makes a Senate into the representative of the elite, whose interests it is to protect. But, given that the United States have abolished such distinctions, why should there be a senate? Publius is embarrased, and admits the difficulty. Like a good philosopher, Publius turns back to history for absolution. He suggests (before Benjamin Constant, who clearly had not read him) that there is a distinction between two kinds of representation. The ancients sought a direct representation of the interests of their constituents, whereas we modern Americans understand that *all offices are representative, but therefore none of them can claim to incarnate the popular will.* It is this notion, which is not just theoretical but rather the expression of the entire debate and politics of independence, that makes it possible to understand the culmination of the revolution in the election of 1800.

The peaceful passing of powers in 1801 reflected the experience that showed that while the Americans were united against their British overlord, they were divided among themselves and were able to recognize that, as Aristotle would have it, deliberation about the good life differs from the necessities involved in the production of mere life. But a crucial test came to the fore in 1803. The peaceful passage had not been so smooth as I just suggested; down to the end, the Federalist allies of Adams had sought to assure their positions of power. Indeed, at the midnight that greeted the day he would leave office, John Adams signed a series of nominations to office. Among them was a certain Marbury. Jefferson's adminstration refused to accept this clearly self-interested and partisan nomination. Marbury went to court. Presided by Jeffersons fellow Virginian, and longtime enemy, John Marshall, the Supreme Court saw the political difficulty, but its decision was based on 40 years of debate around the question of sovereignty. Yes, ruled the court, the Jeffersonians represented the recently elected majority; but that did not mean that their policies incarnated the will of the sovereign people. A temporary majority, ruled the court, does not represent, let alone incarnate, the people. It is the constitution, which defines the sphere within which politics takes place, that is the *symbolic* representation of the sovereign. And the task of the court therefore is not to take sides in a political quarrel but to maintain that constitution by insuring that no party or branch of government can claim it for its own partisan purposes.

As symbolic, the sovereignity of the people can thus be at once one and divided, united in spite of the different interests and interpretations that are the stuff of politics. And the lesson of the American experience of a republican democracy can be generalized in the claim that it is the paradoxical task of *modern* politics (as opposed to the classical vision) to make sure that it remains structured by the tension between that symbolic unity and the different parties that offer competing programs claiming to realize it. In this context, representation does not reduce but enhances democracy because it sets out a model or ideal that by its very nature cannot be incarnated and which therefore appeals to – or, more strongly, demands – the deliberation of participating citizens. Granted, representative government in the America of today has become something rather different. Indeed, the lesson of U.S. history is not defined only by the success of its republican democratic invention. What that history shows, on the contrary, is the difficulty of maintaining such a political form. The basis of the uncertain history of republican democracy can be understood if it is recalled that the philosophical attractiveness of Marx's systematic quest for a total and totalizing theory was based on its formulation as a politics of will. Consonant with the modern vision of a sovereign polity, such a politics of will may have found its limits in our contemporary world. The issues posed by the mixed reality of cosmopolitanism and the need to create some form of international law put into question the volontarist framework on which the state has been based since the Westphalian settlement. A brief discussion of those two issues in the light of the preceding will round out my argument for the necessity of politics by suggesting the contours of what I call *the politics of judgment.*

4. The Principles of the Politics of Judgement

At the outset of this presentation, I said that I had been driven back to philosophical and historical considerations because of the way in which cosmopolitanism had become identified with the rights of man, at the same time that the philosophical interpretation of international law tended toward a form of proceduralism. In both cases, there is no room for politics: it is either replaced by unversal moral imperatives, or its unavoidable, and even desirable, particularity is denied by the deontological assumptions that justice can be reduced to formal modes of regulation. (While this latter point may be rendered moot in some readings of Habermas's legal theory, which does try to build in a vital place for democracy,[8] for the purposes of my argument, that point can be left for later discussion. I would be less generous toward attempts to avoid the problem through notions of "reflexive law," but that too can be left aside for now[9].)

My criticism of these contemporary approaches presupposed a conception of politics, which I left implicit in the preceding discussions of both Marx and the two eighteenth-century democratic revolutions. One further step needs to be taken before I can make explicit the idea of politics that I am claiming to be necessary. The reduction of cosmopolitanism to human rights, and the attempt to create totalizing codes of international law that supersede the particularity of the nation state are not only problematic but, in the last resort, misleading. In the first place, both orientations presuppose a politics of will, either in the form of a morality that is universal in scope, or as a set of procedures that are equally universal in their neutrality. The result is that there is no place for the particular and the plural, and therefore no space for difference and no time for deliberation. It follows, second, that the double reduction neglects the plurality that is essential to both. Our ever-more cosmopolitan world is anything but uniform; in spite of the fears of the old Frankfurt Critical Theorists, its diversity has grown, and it must be taken seriously as such. This would not surprise the author of the classic statement of Enlightenement politics whose essay on "Perpetual Peace" stressed that the creation of a world republic as the implicit horizon that could bring lawful unity to international relations is both undesirable and unrealizable. In its place, he proposed a principle of "hospitality" whose political implications cannot be reduced to a moral imperative. Rather, what is called the crisis of international law does not stem from the absence of a higher authority – a sovereign will – to enforce it. The challenge lies, rather, in determining the matters with which international law can and should be concerned. The answer to that political question depends, however, on a philosophical argument that defines what I've called a *politics of judgement*. It will permit a clearer understanding of the nature of the sovereignty that is put to work in a republican democracy.

The nature of a politics of judgement can be explained normatively (philosophically) by adapting arguments from Kant's third *Critique*, or genetically (historically) by developing the model of a republican democracy in contrast to the democratic republican politics of will that Marx elaborated in the wake of the French revolution. The historical experience can be seen to point beyond its immediate significance to acquire a normative status when it is interpreted in terms of the philosophical claim, whose force it serves to illustrate. In the American experience, this means that the concept of a unified sovereign people whose general will is expressed by the actions of the state is overcome. The popular will was seen to be represented in all branches of the government, and for that very reason to be incarnate in none of them. As a result, the checks and balances among the branches led to the emergence of constantly changing political alliances, permitting new questions to emerge as others were solved (or forgotten). Tocqueville seems to have well understood the *enjeux* of republican democracy when he said he loved democracy not for what it is but for what it makes people do (*fait faire*)[10]. But even as diversity and plurality were insured in this manner, unity was not forgotten; indeed, it was their precondition. The Court's decision in 1803 was the exception that proves the rule of republican democracy. Its affirmation of the national unity as *represented* by the Constitution which is the *symbolic* incarnation of a popular will represented temporarily by the majority government was the explicit articulation of the general, and taken-for-granted understanding of politics in a republican democracy.

A more philosophical formulation of the same experience is suggested by what Kant called *reflective judgement*. The concept of "judgement" should not be taken to imply the passive stance of an observer who has no effect on the situation that is observed. Judgement is an activity[11]. Particulars that cannot be subsumed under pregiven universally valid laws are presented by one or another of the political (or governmental) agents; they are then *re*presented to the public in the form of validity claims to which the public must show its receptivity. As with the development of Marx's work, attention must be paid to both sides, the particularity and the receptivity, each of which can change historically. The task of politics is likewise double. It is necessary to articulate particular claims that cannot be subsumed under generally given forms of law, institutions or technological solutions. These particulars must be presented as demanding a solution that is universal, but one that can come into being only through the cooperation of all the concerned participants. On the other hand, and in the same process, there must be created on the side of the citizenry a receptivity to the proposed solutions. This is where Kant makes use of the notion of a "common sense" or a public opinion that serves to bind together the two poles. It is interesting to note that this idea of a common sense passes through stages of development: Kant stresses that it is a particular common *sense*; it then develops on the side of receptivity to become a *common* sense; and then, finally, it can emerge as a *communal* sense (a *gemeinschaftlicher Sinn*). It is this triple development that explains why judgement is not just a passive observation of a world external to it.

If we return now to actual political history, we can note that when, for whatever reason, the political institutions show themselves to be incapable of fulfilling the task of assuring both the plurality of social interest and the symbolic but effective unity of the polity – as in the years leading to the Civil War, for example – the Supreme Court must again enter the picture. Its role is not to replace public political decision-making but to recreate or reaffirm the symbolic framework of unity against which the formation of political judgement can occur – as was the case, for example, with the Civil Rights decisions of the 1960s. Its philosophical correlate could be shown to lie in an interpretation of Kant's principle of hospitality. The difficulty in elaborating its political translation is suggested by the title of the book in which I first presented the argument for a politics of judgement: *From Marx to Kant*. As opposed to Marx's quest to overcome once and for all the opposition of particularity and universality, Kant's theory of judgement, when suitably integrated into political history[12], offers a phenomenological approach to political life that is capable of confronting the dilemmas from which we began this discussion, cosmopolitism on the one side, and the always frustrated quest to subsume its diversity under a unified system of international law.

The difficulty in maintaining a politics of judgement arises from the fact that, while necessary, such a politics can never be sufficient. And the same holds true for the modern republican democracy, which cannot be – as the young Marx once put it – "the generic constitution... Democracy is content and form... [it is] the resolved mystery of all constitutions." Republican democracy not only permits but makes necessary the constant clash between particular and universal, plurality and unity, private interest and public weal, as well as – against a global world in becoming – the rich diversity of cosmopolitanism and the neutral procedures of international law. The temptation to overcome these tensions is always present, particularly for the heirs of an Enlightenment for which the idea of Progress was a *leitmotif*. This is why the return to Marx and the revolutionary politics of will is not simply a rhetorical flourish that I have used in order to accent the uniqueness of the politics of judgement. What I called the fruitfulness of Marx's systematic project is due to its ability to maintain the tension inherent in modern democratic society. What he could not understand is that the unity sought by his politics of will could be only *symbolic*. Despite this failure, his attempt warns against the attempt to absolutize one or the other of the poles that constitute the political experience of a republican democracy. But it doesn't tell us how to do so. It only warns against treating either international law or cosmopolitanism as real or to-be-realized. The politics of judgement goes a step further, suggesting the need to treat both as symbolic. In this way, the orientation toward a better future that Marx's project shared with the progressive Enlightenment can be maintained. While one cannot be a Marxist, one can be greatful that his totalizing quest to overcome contradiction by means of a politics of will preserves the idea that the future is *not* already written and (*malgré* the *Manifesto*) waiting only for the proper moment to appear. Just this (genetic) politics of will makes possible, and necessary, the (normative) politics of judgement. The symbolic is thereby rended real – that is, actual – because it is made effective (*wirklich, weil wirkend*).

Notes

1. The thesis concerning the "two hundred years of error" is developed first in some of the essays collected in *Political Judgments* (Lanham, Md.: Rowman & Littlefield, 1996). The radical implications of democracy are developed in *The Specter of Democracy* (New York: Columbia University Press, 2002).
2. C.f. *Marx: Aux origines de la pensée critique* (Paris: Michalon, 2001).
3. The concept of a "regime" is tricky. It goes back to the Greek understanding of politics, but it could as well be understood with reference to something like what Marcel Mauss called a "total social fact."
4. The book (Paris: Buchet-Chastel, 2004) tries to recreate the historical-political emergence of a peculiar kind of American democracy, to which I return below. Each chapter has four parts: lived history, history conceptualized, history reflected upon, and history as rethought by successive generations of historians. The three chapters into which the work is divided represent themselves the phases of lived, conceived and reflected history. I will return to the arguments of this book later.
5. This lengthy, incomplete and unpublished manuscript is the first complete outline of the systematic project of *Das Kapital*, which itself manifests the systematic structure by virtue of the triadic structure of its three planned volumes. The first was to treat the "immediate process of production," while the second looked at its mediation through the sphere of circulation, and the third was to treat "the process as a whole." Indeed, a fourth – the theories of surplus value – was intended to represent not only previous and incorrect doctrines but also to show how all theory prior to *Das Kapital* led toward and was summed up in Marx's master work. This dialectical structure is often clearer in Marx's spontaneously written drafts than it is in his later, more polished publications.
   Citations in the pages that follow are indicated by the sign *Gr*, followed by a page number. The translation is from Karl Marx, *Grundrisse*, (New York: Vintage Books, 1973).
6. C.f., Dick Howard, *Aux origines de la pensée politique américaine* (Paris: Buchet-Chastel, 2004).
7. Although this essay was written by Madison, a similar argument is proposed by Hamilton in number 9. Thus, one cannot suppose immediately the existence of ideological distinctions that came out in the elections of 1800.
8. I've tried to emphasize this aspect of Habermas's theory in a chapter of *The Specter of Democracy*, under the title "Habermas's Reorientation of Critical Theory toward Democratic

Theory," and at greater length in "Law and Political Culture," in Dick Howard, *Political Judgments* (Lanham, Md., Rowman & Littlefield, 1996), pp. 171-210.

9. This notion has been developed by students of Habermas. Benhabib, *op. cit.*, gives a brief presentation of the thesis, which she then develops in a more satisfactory (because more political) manner as the notion of "political iterations" through which a particular problem that cannot be resolved politically passes to the level of the court system, which produces a temporary solution that is, then, returned to the political terrain for a new iteration.

10. The concept is found in a chapter whose title confirms the argument made here: "The Activity Present in All Parts of the Political Body of the United States: The Influence that it Exercises on Society." C.f., *De la démocratie en Amérique, I* (Paris: Gallimard, 1961), volume 1, p. 254.

11. Let me stress, as strongly as I can, that what I call a "politics of will" is a voluntarism, which differs radically from the action that is produced or engendered by a politics of judgement. The politics of will paradoxically seeks to put an end to politics, making action by the citizens unnecessary. The practice of such a politics of will becomes at best paternalist but more likely totalitarian in its realization, as I've tried to show in *The Specter of Democracy*.

12. I add this clause because Kant's earlier attempt to passe from philosophy to political history, found in the essay on the "Idea for a Universal History with a Cosmopolitan Purpose," ultimately fails for reasons similar to those that are responsible for Marx's own failure. Kant proposes something like a "politics of will," or what I called in *From Marx to Kant* a "constitutive theory," in order to overcome the dualism that he locates in humanity's "unsocial sociability" – a concept that is not without echoes of Marx's depiction of the proletariat that we discussed above.

Danish Yearbook of Philosophy, Vol. 40 (2005), 57-78

THE EVENT, THE PHENOMENON AND THE REVEALED *

JEAN-LUC MARION

University of Paris IV, Sorbonne

I. What shows itself and what gives itself

Every phenomenon appears, but it appears only to the extent that it shows it-self. Heidegger convincingly demonstrated that the phenomenon is defined as what shows itself in itself and from itself. Still, he left the question of how to think the self at work in what shows itself largely undetermined.[1] How in fact can a phenomenon claim to deploy itself, if a transcendental I constitutes it is an object placed at the disposition of and by the thought that fully penetrates it?

In such a world – the world of technical objects, our world for the most part – phenomena can only reach the rank of objects. Thus their phenomenality is merely borrowed and it is as if they are derived from the intentionality and the intuition that we grant to them. To admit the contrary, that a phenomenon shows itself, one would have to be able to acknowledge it to be a self that ini-tiates its manifestation. The question is then to know whether and how such an initiation of manifestation can befall a phenomenon. We have proposed the following response: a phenomenon can show itself only to the extent that it gives itself first – nothing can show itself unless it gives itself first. Still, as we will see, the reverse is not necessarily true, since what gives itself need not show itself – the given[2] is not always phenomenalized. How then to get a bear-ing on what gives itself? The givenness of self cannot be seen directly, since what can be seen must have shown itself already, or at least, in the case of ob-jects, it must have been shown. If manifestation perhaps proceeds from the given, then the given has to precede it; the given is therefore anterior to mani-festation. In other words, the given is not yet implicated in the space of visibil-ity and so, strictly speaking, unseen. Therefore, we could not access the given, the movement through which the phenomenon gives itself, by outlining the visibility of what possibly shows itself there, assuming of course that a non-objective phenomenality could manifest itself that way. Only one solution re-mains: to try to locate, in the very space of manifestation, the regions where phenomena show themselves, instead of simply letting themselves be shown as objects. Or, to isolate regions where the self of what shows itself testifies indisputably of the thrust, the pressure, and, so to speak, the impact of what gives itself. The self of what shows itself would then manifest indirectly that it gives itself in a more fundamental sense. This same self, located in the phenomenon showing itself, would come from the original self of that which gives itself. Better: the self of phenomenalization would then manifest indirectly the self of the given, because the one would employ the other and ultimately coincide with it.

Yet how to detect such an ascension from the phenomenalizing self to the giving self? Which phenomena retain the trace of their donation in them, to the point that their mode of phenomenalization not only gives access to their originary self, but also renders it incontestable? Consider the following hypothesis: the phenomena in question have the character of an event. In fact, though the event seems to be a phenomenon like any other, it can be distinguished from objective phenomena in that it is not a result of a process of production. The event is not a product, determined and foreseen, predictable on the basis of its causes, and reproducible through the repetition of these causes. On the contrary, in happening the event testifies of an unpredictable origin, arising due to largely unknown or even absent causes, to causes that are at least unassignable, such that one does not know how to reproduce it, for its constitution has no sense. Still, it could be objected that such events are rare, that their very unpredictability renders them unsuitable for analyzing manifestation, in short that they provide no solid ground for an inquiry into the given. Could this seemingly obvious objection be challenged? We shall try to do so, choosing a most trivial example, namely this room, the Salle des Actes of the Catholic Institute, where today's academic meeting is held.

Even this auditorium appears in the mode of an event. Do not object that it lets itself be seen in the manner of an object – four walls, a false ceiling hiding a balcony, a podium, a certain number of seats, all available in the manner of permanent and subsistent beings that exist, waiting for us to inhabit them and use them or for us to certify their subsistence. For, curiously, this permanence in waiting signifies the opposite of objective availability.

(a) According to the past. As always already there, available for our arrival and usage, this hall imposes itself on us as preceding us, being without us even if for us. It appears to our view as an unexpected, unpredictable fact, originating in an uncontrollable past. The surprise of this appearance as unexpected does not apply only to the rooms of this particular Romanesque palace, often passed by in the walks about town of an ignorant tourist or in the hurried march of a blasé inhabitant of the Eternal City, but which, sometimes in response to an exceptional invitation, on entering we suddenly discover in all its unpredictable and, until now, unknown splendor. The surprise applies equally well to the Salle des Actes – already there, emerging from a past that we ignore. Redecorated many times thanks to now forgotten restoration projects, weighed down with a history exceeding our memory (could it be a converted cloister?), it forces itself upon me when it appears. It is not so much that I enter this room as it is that the room itself comes to me, engulfs me, and imposes itself upon me. This "already" testifies of the event.

(b) According to the present. Here, the nature of the event of the phenomenon of this hall shines forth. For it is no longer a question of the Salle des Actes as such, in general, subsisting as an indifferent vacuity between this or that occasion that fills it with an undifferentiated public. It is a question of this Salle this evening, filled for this occasion, to hear these speakers on this topic. This evening the Salle des Actes becomes a hall – in the theatrical sense of a good or bad hall. It becomes a scene – in the theatrical sense that this or that actor can first fill it, to then keep the attention of the audience. Finally, it is a question of a hall, where what comes to pass are neither the walls nor the stones, neither the spectators nor the orators, but the intangible event that their words will take hold of, making it understood or spoiling it. This moment will certainly insert itself amongst other academic meetings, other conferences, other university ceremonies, but it will never be repeated as such. This evening, devoted to this topic and not any other, among us and no others, an absolutely unique, irreproducible and largely unpredictable event is being played out – after all, at the precise moment that I say "the precise moment," neither you, nor the presiding dean, nor I, none of us knows yet whether it will turn out to be a success or a failure. What appears at this precise moment under our eyes escapes all constitution: having been organized with clear, friendly, intellectual, and social intentions, it shows itself of itself from itself nevertheless. In this "self" of its phenomenality is announced the self of that which gives itself. The "this time, once and for all" testifies then also to the self of the phenomenon.

(c) In the future. Even after the event, no witness, however knowledgeable, attentive, and backed up by documents he or she might be, can describe what is happening at the moment. The event of this public oral presentation, made possible by a consenting audience and a benevolent institution, engages not only material means – itself impossible to describe exhaustively, stone by stone, epoch by epoch, attendee by attendee – but also by an undefined intellectual framework. After all, I must explain what I say and what I mean to say, from where I say it, with what presuppositions I begin, from what texts, from what personal and spiritual problems. It would also be necessary to describe the motivations of each listener: their expectations; their deceptions; their agreements, masked in silence or exaggerated by polemic. Then, in order to describe what kind of event has happened in this "hall," this Salle des Actes, it would be necessary to follow the consequences for the individual and collective evolution of all the participants, the main speaker included – which fortunately is impossible. Such a hermeneutic would deploy itself without end and in no defined network.[3] No constitution of an object, exhaustive and reproducible, can be at work here. The "without end" shows that the event arose from itself, that its phenomenality arose from the self of its givenness.

This opening analysis, precisely because it is based on a phenomenon that is, at first sight, simple and banal, assures us that showing-itself can give indirect access to the self of that which gives itself. The event of this "hall," the Salle des Actes, makes a phenomenon appear before us that not only neither arises out of our initiative, nor responds to our expectation, nor can ever be reproduced, but which above all gives itself to us from its own self, to the point that it affects us, changes us, almost produces us. We can never stage an event (nothing would be more ridiculously contradictory than the supposed "organization of the event"); rather, it stages us[4] out of the initiative of its own self by giving itself to us. It stages us in the scene opened by its givenness.

II. The event as the self of the given phenomenon

This analysis, however rigorous it may have been, encounters a difficulty or at least something strange: it considers as an event what at first sight is an object, in this case, the hall. On what basis can an object be interpreted as an event – a hall as a "hall"? If we follow that line of thinking, in the end could not every object be described as an event? Should not a more reasonable distinction be maintained between these two concepts? And what is gained from such an interpretation? After all, the object certainly belongs to the sphere of phenomenality, yet it is not evident that the phenomenon still comes under it.

To answer these sensible objections one must undoubtedly turn the question around and ask, on the contrary, how can the essential and original event character of phenomena (even of the most banal type, like the one we have just described) grow blurred, attenuate, and disappear, to the point that it appears as no more than an object? One should not ask: up to what point can one legitimately think the phenomenon as an event? Instead, the question is: why can one miss phenomenality by reducing it to objectivity?

To reply to this question, we can find inspiration in Kant. The first of the four headings that organize the categories of understanding and so impose onto phenomena the quadruple seal of objectivity refers to quantity. Kant points out that, to become an object, every phenomenon must possess a quantity, a magnitude. Given this magnitude, the totality of the phenomenon equals and results from the sum total of its parts. From that follows another decisive feature: it can and must be possible to anticipate the object on the basis of the sum of the parts that compose it, such that it is always "intuited in advance [schon angeschaut][5] as an aggregate (the sum of parts given in advance [vorher angeschaut])."[6] That certainly signifies that the magnitude of the phenomenon can, by right, always be modeled in a finite quantity, and so be inscribed in a real space or be transcribed (by means of models, parameters and encoding) into an imaginary space. That signifies above all that the phenomenon is inscribed in a space that we can always know in advance by summing its parts. This hall has a quantity that results from the sum of its parts – these walls delimit its volume and indicate also other nonextended parameters (its fabrication and maintenance cost, occupancy rate, etc.) that specify budgetary costs and its pedagogical use. In principle, no place is left in it for the least surprise: what appears will always inscribe itself in what the sum of these parameters permits to foresee already. The hall is foreseen before it is actually seen – confined in its quantity, defined through its parts, brought to a halt, so to say, by the measurements that precede it and await its empirical execution (its construction). This reduction of the hall to its foreseeable quantity turns it into an object, before and in which we pass as if there were nothing else to be seen in it, nothing other than what can already be envisaged on the basis of its construction plan. The same applies to all technical objects: we no longer see them, we no longer need to see them, since we foresee them far in advance. And we succeed in using them all the better if we can foresee them without being preoccupied with seeing them. We only need to begin to see them when we can no longer or not yet foresee them, that is to say, when we can no longer or not yet use them (in other words, when they break down or when we are learning to use them). Within the limits of typical technical usage, we thus have no need to see objects; it suffices us to foresee them. We thus reduce them to the rank of second order, common law, phenomena, deprived of full, that is autonomous and disinterested, appearance. They appear transparent to us, in the neutral light of objectivity. Of what is a phenomenon foreseen and not seen, turned into an object, deprived? When we style it a foreseen phenomenon, is it not this very foresight that disqualifies it as a full phenomenon? What does foresight mean here? That in the object everything remains seen in advance, that nothing unexpected will turn up – costs, occupancy, utility, etc. The object remains a phenomenon that has expired because it appears as something that has always already expired: nothing new can happen to it, since, more radically, under the regard that constitutes it, it appears as what cannot happen at all. The object appears as the shadow of the event that we deny in it.

Still, we could inverse the analysis and move from the object, the transparent phenomenon deprived of any ability to happen, to its original phenomenality, governed part and parcel by eventiality [l'événementialité] – following the rule of essence that what truly shows itself must first give itself. We have in fact already accomplished this move from the object to the event by describing the common law phenomenon – this "hall," that is precisely not the Salle des Actes – as a triple event, according to the "already" of its facticity, the "this time, once and for all" of its realization, and the "without end" of its hermeneutics. It remains then to return to the description of the evential character of phenomenality in general, referring from now on to phenomena that can unquestionably be thematized as events. First, collective phenomena are called by the title of event ("historical": political revolution, war, natural disaster, cultural or sport event, etc.), and they satisfy at least three requirements.

(a) They cannot be repeated identically and thus they show themselves to be identical only to themselves: irreproducibility, hence irreversibility.

(b) They can be assigned neither a unique cause nor exhaustive explanation; the number of causes and possible explanations is indefinite and increases in proportion to the hermeneutic that historians, sociologists, economists, etc. can develop to their purposes – exceeding the number of effects and facts of any system of causes.

(c) They cannot be foreseen, since their partial causes remain not only insufficient, but are discovered only after the effect has been accomplished. It follows that their possibility, impossible to foresee, remains strictly speaking an impossibility with regard to the system of previously classified causes. Importantly enough, these three requirements do not refer exclusively to collective phenomena; they also define private or intersubjective phenomena.

Let us analyze an exemplary and yet banal case, that of Montaigne's friendship for La Boétie. The canonical determinants of a phenomenon as an event, which we developed elsewhere, can be found in it.[7] Friendship with another forces me, first of all, to have regard towards him, a regard that does not follow my intentionality toward him, but submits itself to the point of view that he has toward me, thus placing me at the exact point where his own intention awaits to expose me. This anamorphosis is described precisely by Montaigne: "We looked for each other before we saw one another." To look for themselves means that, like rivals who provoke and eye each other up and down, each tried to place himelf there where the look of the other could come to rest on him. In other words, "It is the I-don't-know-what quintessence of this union that, having seized my will, made it plunge and lose itself in his." I take for myself his point of view on me, without reducing it to my point of view on him; and thus it happens to me. Second, the event of this friendship happens all at once, unforeseen and without a warning, in the shape of an unexpected and syncopated arrival: "At our first meeting, we found ourselves so absorbed, so familiar, so committed one to the other, that nothing appeared to us so close as the other." Thus it is an always "already" accomplished fact that its facticity, "by chance during a great feast and city festival," renders it irreversible rather than weakening it. Third, the phenomenon that gives itself gives nothing other than itself; its ultimate meaning remains inaccessible because it is reduced to the accomplished fact, to its incidence. This accident does not indicate any substance; if it signifies more than itself, the surplus remains as unknowable as that "order from heaven" that alone inspires it. From this follows the last feature that characterizes most perfectly the eventiality of the phenomenon: we can assign it neither cause nor reason; or rather, no other reason or cause than itself, in the pure energy of its unquestionable happening: "If pushed to say why I loved him, I feel that nothing could express this but saying, because it was him, because it was me."[8] The phenomenon of friendship thus shows itself only insofar as, as a pure and perfect event, its phenomenality forces itself upon the mode of being of the event so that it gives itself without question or reserve.

In this way the eventiality governing every phenomenon, even the most objective in appearance, demonstrates without exception that what shows itself can only do so in virtue of a strictly and eidetically phenomenological self, which guarantees only that it gives itself and that, in return, it proves that its phenomenalization presupposes its givenness as such and from itself.

III. The time of the self

Consider the result: the self of what shows itself, that is to say the phenomenon, testifies, by its universal and intrinsic eventual character, that it gives itself originarily. Does that not lead to a banal conclusion that every phenomenon, even the intuitively poor or common law object, is temporal? In that case, would we not simply return to a position that is, quite classically, Kantian? Undoubtedly – if we were to accept two inadmissible corollaries of his critique.

First, this one: temporality serves only to permit the synthesis of phenomena as objects, thus working to assure permanence in presence. Now, our analysis establishes exactly the contrary: temporality originarily brings about the happening of occurences as accomplished fact, with neither reason nor cause and by imposing an anamorphosis. In short, it allows phenomenality to be understood under the mode of event, contrary to all objectivity, which becomes at best a residual case, provisionally permanent, illusorily subsistent. Temporality does not work for the sake of objects, but in favor of the event, which undoes and overdetermines the object, which, to repeat, is the simple illusion of an atemporal event.

The other corollary: temporality as internal sense belongs to sensibility and only operates by orienting the subject towards the synthesis of known objects; still, the transcendental I, the operator of this synthesis (of syntheses), even though it puts temporality to work in a masterly manner, is not itself defined strictly as such according to this temporality. Even if we suppose that phenomena temporalized as objects preserve a trace of eventiality (which is open to question), still the transcendental I itself, however temporalizing it might be, absolutely does not phenomenalize itself as an event. And it does not for a reason that is absolutely determinative: it never phenomenalizes itself, does not appear amongst other phenomena, excluded as it is from the phenomenality it produces. Having said that, we cannot overcome the Kantian objection with only negative arguments. To truly overcome it, it will be necessary to identify phenomena temporalized eidetically as events; temporalized in such a way that they provoke the ego to phenomenalize itself according to this unique eventiality. Can we adduce such a phenomenon?

A premier case of such a phenomenon presents itself: death, a phenomenon that can only be phenomenalized in its coming to pass, for outside of this passage it cannot properly be; it only appears then to the extent that it comes to pass; if it didn't, it could never be. Death can only show itself by giving itself as an event. It could never let itself be seen otherwise. Still, when it happens, what does it show of itself? Is it not subject to the classical aporia according to which, as long as I am, death is not, and when it happens, I am no longer there to see it? Does it not provide only the illusion of an event, the illusion that a phenomenon gives itself? To reply we must provide a somewhat more precise description and distinguish between the death of the other and my own.

The death of the other appears to the extent that it comes to pass, but it consists precisely in the pure and simple passage, itself not real, from the state of a living being to that of a corpse. This passage cannot be seen directly. Unlike the two states it traverses, as a phenomenon the death of the other lasts only the instant of the passage (even if the funeral ceremony tries to make it last and does so for the very reason that the passage lasted only a moment). The death of the other shows itself only in a flash and it gives itself only in withdrawing – by removing the living other from us. It is a pure phenomenon, to be sure, yet too pure to show itself and so give itself as a perfect event. And this is even more true since this flash of event does not involve my ego, since, by enclosing me in my residual life, the death of the other bars all access to both the other and to death.

My own death involves me completely, to be sure, and it also appears only in coming to pass, and thus as an event testifying to a phenomenal givenness. However, an obvious aporia compromises its relevance: if death comes to pass upon me (supposing that a phenomenon manifests itself in this passage), insofar as I pass away together with it, I could never see the event. Certainly, this aporia poses a threat only from the point of view of one who has not yet experienced this passage, who does not know whether it will annihilate me or "change" me (1 Corinthians 15:52). Thus, this aporia of my death only matters to one who, like all us of here, has not yet died. We are ignorant as to whether that which gives death is an event or a nihilation of phenomenality. In fact, the human condition is primarily characterized neither by death (animals and civilizations die as well) nor by the consciousness of ending in death, but by the ignorance of what happens (or shows itself) to me at the moment when death comes upon me. My death does not then place me before an effectivity nor a passage. Rather, it places me before a simple possibility – the possibility of impossibility. And this possibility of impossibility, which will necessarily give itself, retains up until the end the possibility of not showing itself, of not showing anything. Hence the event of my death, the closest, the least far away, from which only one heart beat separates me, remains inaccessible to me by the excess in it (and it is, provisionally, at least inevitable), by the excess of its pure donation to phenomenality. There too we are surely dealing with a pure phenomenon, but one too pure to show itself and so to give itself as a perfect event. This phenomenon, which deserves the title of an event and which involves me in it radically because it gives itself, nevertheless withdraws as a phenomenon that shows itself.

How can we proceed? Let us return to the phenomenon itself: it gives itself in that it shows itself, yet only insofar as the manifestation occurs in it in the mode of a happening that falls before my gaze as an accomplished fact (an incident) that it appropriates (anamorphosis). Obviously these determinations refer to time, which the event radically presupposes. Yet does not the event involve time as one of its elements or conditions? Certainly not. For time itself first happens in the mode of an event. Husserl saw that, defining time as starting from an "original impression," that, as a "source point," continuously arises in and as the pure present, and that, precisely because it occurs, does not cease to pass into the no-longer-present, a time retained by retention before sinking into the past.[9] The present arises as first and the first comes to pass as pure event – unpredictable, irreversible, irreproducible as such, immediately past and deprived of cause or reason. It alone escapes objectivity, even though it makes it possible, because it is absolutely excluded from all constitution: "The originary impression is a non-modifiable absolute, the original source for all consciousness and being to come."[10] Here the movement of that which gives itself is accomplished and almost no possibility of appearing is left to that which shows itself, since the originary impression changes immediately and, as soon as it arises, lives continually in retention. Still, unlike death, this excess of givenness does not prevent an event from being effectively and even sensibly accomplished, since the originary impression does not cease to reappear from the absolute unseen, from the shadow out of which it emerges. The originary impression gives itself to be seen as a pure event relentlessly brought to life through indefinite and unconditional birth. From the "source point," givenness unremittingly at work, what hardly shows itself (this instant) is born from each instant of that which gives itself completely (the originary impression).

Birth – here we have a phenomenon that shows itself truly in the mode of what gives itself, the phenomenon that is properly evential. The question is how to understand my birth showing itself as a phenomenon, since, properly

speaking, I have never actually seen it with my own eyes and, in order to re-
constitute it, I must rely on eye witnesses or administrative decisions? Though
it takes place without me and even, strictly speaking, before me, it should not
be able to show itself (if it showed itself) to anybody other than me. Still, I
consider it a phenomenon, since I continuously intend it (I want to know who
I am and where I come from, I search for personal identity, etc.) and I fulfil
these intentions with quasi-intuitions (second hand memories, direct and indirect testimony, etc.). My birth appears even as a privileged phenomenon, since
a significant part of my life is devoted to reconstituting it, giving it sense, and
responding to its silent call. Still, in principle I cannot see this unquestionable
phenomenon directly. This aporia could be formalized by saying that my birth
shows me precisely that my origin cannot be shown, in short that it only attests
to the originary non-originality of the origin [l'originaire non-originelleité de
l'origine].[11] This must be understood in a double sense. Either my birth happens before I can see and receive it, in which case I am not present at my own
origin, or my birth, my origin is in itself nothing originary but flows from an
indefinite series of events and appearances (sumque vel a parentibus produc-
tus).[12] However, to describe this aporia is not yet to resolve it. It remains to be
understood how a phenomenon that does not show itself (and in a sense it does
show itself well through numerous intermediaries) not only affects me as if it
did show itself, but also affects me more radically than any other, since it alone
determines me, defines my ego, even produces it. Put otherwise: if an origin
cannot in general show itself, all the less can an origin dispossessed of its orig-
inarity. How then does this originary non-originality happen to me – since it
happens to me, has happened to me, I come to it – if it remains necessarily in-
demonstrable? It happens to me exactly in that it happens, and happens [ad-
venir] only in that it endows me with a future [l'avenir]. My birth is not called
a phenomenon (that of the non-originary origin) because it shows itself, but
because, in the very absence of any direct monstration, it comes to pass as an
event that was never present and always already dated [passé], but never out-
dated [dépassé] – in fact, always to-come. My birth does phenomenalize itself,
but as a pure event, unpredictable, irreproducible, exceeding all cause, and
making the impossible possible (that is to say, my always new life), surpassing
all expectation, all promise, and all prediction. This phenomenon, which is accomplished in a perfect reduction of that which shows itself, thus testifies in an
exceptional and paradigmatic way that its phenomenality flows directly from
the fact that it gives itself.

We thus find what we have been looking for: all that shows itself not only gives itself, but gives itself as an event according to a temporality that is itself evential, to the point that, in exceptional cases (birth), a phenomenon directly succeeds in giving itself without showing itself.

In fact, a number of characteristics justify the phenomenological privilege granted to birth:

(a) The phenomenon of birth gives itself directly without showing itself directly because it comes to pass as an event par excellence (an origin originally non-originary). Nevertheless, this excellence follows from the fact that it gives me to myself when it gives itself. It phenomenalizes itself by affecting me, but it affects me not only by giving me to myself, but (since without it I would not yet be there to be affected by it) by giving a myself a me, which receives itself from what it receives.[13]

(b) From the beginning, the phenomenon of birth takes to its height the inclusion of the ego in eventiality by founding that ego in an exemplary way as the given-to[14]: the one that receives itself from what it receives. The phenomenon of birth exemplifies the phenomenon in general – something can phenomenalize itself only to the extent that it gives itself. However, at the same time, it institutes the given-to (originarily a posteriori since it receives itself from what it receives), the first phenomenon (making possible the reception of all others).

(c) Thus, the phenomenon of birth gives itself as a full-fledged saturated phenomenon (or paradox). In effect, its event, the first originating impression and so more originary than any other instant, makes possible an indefinite, indescribable, and unpredictable series of originating impressions to come – those that accumulate in the span of my life and that define me until the end of my life. In this way birth opens the course of innumerable temporal intuitions, for which I unceasingly, but always too late, will seek to find significations, concepts, and noeses that will inevitably remain insufficient. I will always try to find the words to tell (myself) what will happen to me, or rather, what will have already happened to me, without being able to adequately explain, understand, or constitute it when it happens. The excess of intuition over intention bursts forth from my birth on – and moreover, I will speak not so much because I have intended silently, but above all after hearing others speak. Language is heard first and spoken only afterwards. The origin certainly remains inaccessible, not because of its deficiency, but because the first phenomenon already saturates every intention with intuitions. The origin, which refuses to show itself, does not, however, give itself through poverty (Derrida), but through excess, thus determining the organization of all the givens to come. That is to say, that nothing shows itself unless it first gives itself.

IV. Is the reduction to the given self-contradictory?

Let us take it as granted that the phenomenon, considered in its radical evential character, reduces to the given. Such a given, especially if it is thought in terms of my birth, insofar as it can give itself as a spectacle of which I would be a spectator (whether disinterested or not does not matter here) without showing itself directly, is accomplished as a saturated phenomenon. It is a saturated phenomenon that, in the event, strikes an ego which, under that blow [coup], becomes a given-to. In effect, such an event gives itself at a stroke [coup]: it leaves one speechless; it leaves one with no way to escape it; in the end, it leaves one without the choice either to refuse or to voluntarily accept it. Its accomplished fact cannot be discussed, nor avoided, nor decided. It is not even a question of a kind of violence, since violence implies something arbitrary and, so, an arbiter and an already given space of freedom. It is a question of pure phenomenological necessity: since the event always already gives itself, its givenness already bygone and necessarily contingent, as in the case of the birth phenomenon or originary impression, it makes manifest the self of that which gives itself. It testifies that this phenomenon and, by derivation, all other phenomena can give themselves in the strict sense, for it proves that, as a pure event, it makes such a self available. Not only does the event give itself in itself (canceling the retreat of the thing in itself), but it gives itself from itself and so as a self.

The stakes at risk in this analysis should not be underestimated: if the self belongs to the phenomenon, no ego can continue to pretend to claim, in first place and first instance, ipseity, the self. Does not the ego of Descartes attain its self in reply to the nescio quis that pertains to it, whether as the deceiver or, rather, as the almighty? Does not Dasein arrive at its ipseity by an anticipatory resolution that makes possible the event of nothingness, which it tears out from the ontic? We contend that the attempts, however grandiose they might be, to assign the status of the first self to the ego, in other words, to give the ego transcendental dignity, manage to do no more than to underline the radical primacy of the self of an event, whatever it is (whether an entity in the world, an entity out of the world, or the totality of entities [l'étant en totalité]) and whatever it is not. If only for the sake of being concerned, one has to recognize that if the phenomenon truly gives itself, it necessarily confiscates the function and the role of the self in the process, thus conceding to the ego only a secondary and derived me. And we explicitly draw this conclusion in challenging the pretension of every I to a transcendental function or, what is the same, the pretension of a possible transcendental I as the ultimate foundation of the experience of phenomena. Said otherwise: the ego, dispossessed of its transcendental purple,[15] must be admitted as it receives itself, as a given-to: the one who receives itself from what it receives, the one to whom what gives itself from a first self – every phenomenon – gives a secondary me, that of reception and response. Certainly the ego keeps all the privileges of subjectivity, except for the transcendental pretension of origin.

The *ego* is found only in being one to whom is given, endowed with a given me and given to receive what gives itself. Among the possible objections against such a diminutio ipseitatis of the ego, one demands our attention more than the rest because it directly puts into question the phenomenological claim of our enterprise. In fact, for all of phenomenology, the reduction functions, whether explicitly (Husserl) or implicitly (Heidegger, Levinas, Henry, Derrida), as its touchstone; it is nonnegotiable because it is not one concept among others, nor a doctrine to be discussed, but an operation that redirects the appearance of appearing to the appearing of phenomena as such. Now, every reduction calls for an agency that operates it – a transcendental I or its equivalent *(Dasein,* the face of the other, flesh). Now the reduction of appearance to the given that we claim to accomplish deviates dangerously from the two other principal reductions that it tries to overcome. First of all, because it does not simply reduce the phenomenon to its constituted object character (Husserl) nor to its being-an-entity in being (Heidegger), but ultimately to the given showing itself insofar as it gives itself – thus establishing the given as an ultimate term and irreducible by any other reduction. And it deviates all the more dangerously because this third reduction leads to the given only by reducing the I to the derived and secondary level of the given-to. This reduction of the I to the given-to would matter little if it were only a question of a new title and not of another function – the function of receiving oneself from what gives itself and no longer playing the transcendental role, in short, the function of no longer determining the conditions of possibility of experience, in other words of phenomenality. Now, the reduction, whose task is precisely to change the conditions of the possibility of phenomenality, requires such an a priori I (or its transcendental equivalent) and so seems unable to be satisfied with a given-to, something that is by definition a posteriori. In short, the reduction of phenomenon to the givenness of what gives itself, going so far as to disqualify the transcendental I in a pure and simple given-to, becomes a performative contradiction – it is deprived of the very operator of givenness that it nevertheless claims to make manifest by reduction.

Such a difficulty cannot be resolved all at once. Still, the following needs to be said: if all reductions require an operator that takes us from the appearance of the appearing to the full appearing of the phenomena, then this operator itself is modified in an essential way by the reduction it operates. For Husserl, the phenomenological reduction (not to evoke others that would, no doubt, yield the same result), reduces things of the world to their conscious experience, in view of constituting their intentional objects; still, the I reduces itself to its pure immanence ("conscious region"), locating the ensemble of its empirical ego in the transcendence of the "world region."[16] Thus, the I becomes transcendental in the phenomenological sense, since it gets reduced to itself and removed from the natural world by renouncing the natural attitude. For Heidegger, the phenomenological reduction of worldly objects (whether subsistent or common) to their status of beings that are seen according to their diversified ways of being can be brought about only by Dasein, the only being in which there is a question of being. Not only is it necessary that Dasein accomplishes itself as such, and so appropriate its unique way of being and rid itself of the inauthentic mode (that of the "One," which pretends to understand itself as an intra-worldly being). The Dasein must then reduce itself to itself – to the status of a being that transcends all other intra-worldly beings in virtue of being itself; this is accomplished during the experience of anxiety. The disappearance of all anthropological determinations (flesh, sexuality, ideology, etc.), with which some have naively reproached Being and Time, attests precisely to this modification of "man" into a Dasein that turns the reduction onto its agent.

Without trying to compare what cannot be compared, we would say, nevertheless, that the same applies to the third reduction. It is first of all the question of reducing all that claims to appear – object, being, appearance, etc. – to a given. For the formula "as much reduction as givenness" in fact postulates that what the natural attitude accepts with no further ado as a given often is not given yet; or, inversely, that what it finds problematic is in fact absolutely given. It is a question, then, of tracing the necessary connection by which "what shows itself must first of all give itself" and of giving all the weight to the self, by which only can givenness validate manifesta- tion. Yet how can we imagine that the person, whoever it might be, who makes the reduction to the given and takes "self-showing" back to "self-giv- ing" by describing the phenomenon as pure event (thus also as anamorpho- sis, happening, accomplished fact, incident), could leave his own identity un- interrogated, much less keep the identities that correspond so closely to the two preceding reductions? How could he claim to define the conditions of possibility of the experience of phenomena, to which he comes precisely by the third reduction, recognizing that they only show themselves in virtue of their self, such that he reveals himself in the event in which they give them- selves and such that he himself establishes the proper conditions of manifes- tation? If the result of the third reduction, that the phenomenon gives itself from itself, is to be maintained, then the ego can no longer have any tran- scendental pretense. The reduction is not so much compromised, but the re- verse. It is realized as in him whom it makes possible, the given-to. The giv- en-to does not compromise the reduction to the given, but confirms it by transferring the self from itself to the phenomenon.

This argument sets a second in motion. The given-to, fallen out of the tran- scendental rank and the spontaneity or activity that it implies, does not for that turn into passivity or into an empirical me. In fact, the given-to tran- scends passivity as much as activity, because, liberated from the transcenden- tal purple, it annuls the very distinction between the transcendental I and the empirical me.

But what third term can there be between activity and passivity, transcen- dentality and empiricity?

Recall the definition of the given-to: that which receives itself from what it receives. The given-to is characterized therefore by reception. To be sure, re- ception implies passive receptivity, but it also requires active capacity; for the capacity (capacitas), in order to grow to the measure of to maintain its happen- ing, must put itself to work – the work of the given to be received, the work on itself to receive. The work that the given demands of the given-to, each time and as long as it gives itself, explains why the given-to does not receive once and for all (at birth), but does not cease to receive at the event of each given. Still, this reception can really free the given-to from the dichotomies that in- carcerate metaphysical subjectivity only if we understand more clearly its proper phenomenological function. Put otherwise: if the given-to no longer constitutes phenomena, if it is content to receive the pure given and receive it-self from it, then what act, what operation, and what role can it still assume in phenomenality itself?

However, in posing this objection to the given-to, we mark an essential gap, that between the given and phenomenality. We repeat what we often glimpsed before: if all that which shows itself must first give itself, then it does not suf-fice that the given give itself in order to show itself, since sometimes the givenness almost obscures the manifestation. The given-to precisely has the function of measuring in itself the gap between the given – which never ceas-es to impose itself upon it and – and phenomenality – which can only be real-ized to the extent that the reception succeeds in phenomenalizing, or rather lets it phenomenalize itself. This operation, phenomenalizing the given, reverts properly to the given-to in virtue of its difficult privilege of constituting the only given in which the visibility of all other givens happens. The given-to re-veals the given as phenomenon.

V. The revealed

From here on, it is a question of understanding how the given-to reveals (phe-nomenalizes as an event) the given – and how far it does so.

Let us consider first of all the revealed in a strictly phenomenological sense. First, the given obtained by the reduction: it can be described as that which Husserl called "lived experience," Erlebnis. Now – and this crucial point is of-ten forgotten – as such, the lived experience does not show itself, but remains invisible by default. For lack of better words, one can say that it affects me, im-poses itself on me, and weighs on what one could dare to call my conscious-ness (precisely because it does not have yet a clear and distinct consciousness of whatever there is when it receives the pure given). As lived experience, the given remains a stimulus, an excitation, hardly information; the given-to re-ceives it, even though it does not show itself at all. How does the given some-times succeed in passing from being unseen to being seen? There is no ques-tion here of invoking physiological or psychological considerations, not only due to a lack of knowledge of these subjects, but also in principle: before ex-plaining a process, we must first identify it, and the process wherein the visible arises out of the unseen belongs properly to phenomenology. Following that line of thought, one can take the risk of saying that the given, unseen yet re-ceived, projects itself onto the given-to (consciousness, if one prefers) as on a screen; all the power of that given crashes, as it were, onto this screen, imme-diately provoking a double visibility.

Certainly, the visibility of the given, the impact of which was invisible until then, explodes and is broken down into outlines, the first visibles. One could also think of the model of the prism, which captures the white light, up till then invisible, and breaks it down into the spectrum of primary colors, rendered light finally visible. The given-to phenomenalizes by receiving the given, pre-cisely because it is an obstacle to the given; it stands in its way, bringing it to a halt in making it a screen and fixing it in a frame. When the given-to receives the given, it receives it with all the vigor, or even the violence, of a goalkeeper defending against the incoming ball, of a defender blocking a return of volley, of a midfielder returning a winning pass. Screen, prism, frame – the given-to collects the impact of the pure unseen given, in retaining the momentum in or-der to, so to speak, transform its longitudinal force into a spread-out, plane, open surface. With this operation – precisely reception – the given can begin to show itself, starting with outlines of visibility that it conceded to the given-to, or rather that it received from it.

However, the visibility arising from the given makes the visibility of the given-to arise as well. In fact, the given-to does not see itself before receiving the impact of the given. Deprived of the transcendental purple, the given-to no longer precedes the phenomenon, nor does it any longer "accompany" it as a thought already in place; since it receives itself from what it receives, the giv-en-to does not precede the phenomenon and certainly not by a visibility that pre-exists the unseen of the given. In fact, the given-to does not show itself more than the given – its screen or its prism remains perfectly unseen as long as the impact of a given upon it does not suddenly illuminate it; or rather, since properly speaking there is no given-to without this reception, the impact gives rise, for the first time, to the screen onto which it crashes, just as it creates the prism across which it is decomposed. In short, the given-to phenomenalizes it-self by means of the operation through which it phenomenalizes the given.

Thus, the given reveals itself to the given-to by revealing the given-to to it-self. Each phenomenalizes the other as the revealed, which is characterized by this essential phenomenal reciprocity, where seeing implies the modification of the seer by the seen as much as of the seen by the seer. The given-to func-tions as the revelator of the given and the given as the revelator of the given-to – the revelator being understood here in the photographic sense.[17] Perhaps we could take the risk of saying that the philosophical paradox of quantum physics concerning the interdependence of the object and the observer applies, by analogy, to all of phenomenality without exception. But can we still speak here of "phenomenality without exception"? Have we not previously conceded that, though all that shows itself first gives itself, the reverse does not apply, since all that gives itself does not succeed in showing itself? In fact, far from entangling ourselves in a new aporia, we have just found a way out of it. For, if the given shows itself only by being blocked and spreading itself on the screen that the given-to has become for it, if the given-to must be and can be the only one capable of transforming an impact into visibility, then the extent of phenomenalization depends on the resistance of the given-to to the brute shock of the given. By resistance we mean resistance in the sense, suggestive because it is ordinary, of electricity: in a circuit when one restricts the free movement of electrons – whether by design or accidentally – then a part of their energy is dissipated as heat or light. In this way the resistance transforms the unseen movement into phenomenalized light and heat. The greater the resistance to the impact of the given (first of all, lived experiences, intuitions), the more that phenomenological light shows itself. Resistance – the proper function of the given-to – becomes the index of the transmutation of that which gives itself into that which shows itself. The more the intuitive given increases its pressure, the greater resistance is necessary for the given-to to reveal a phenomenon. From this follows the inevitable and logical hypothesis of saturated phenomena – so saturated with given intuitions that no place is left for corresponding significations and noeses. Faced with such partially non-visible phenomena (except in the mode of bedazzlement), only the resistance of the given-to can transmute, up to a certain point, the excess of givenness into a fitting monstration, namely an immeasurable one.

This opens a place for a phenomenological theory of art: the painter makes visible as a phenomenon what no one has ever seen, because, in each case he or she is the first to succeed in resisting the given enough to make it show itself – and then in a phenomenon accessible to all. A great painter never invents anything, as if the given were missing. On the undergoes resistance to this excess, until it gives up its visibility to him (as one makes restitution). Rothko resists what he received as a violent given – too violent for anyone but him – by phenomenalizing it on the screen of spread-out color: "I imprisoned the most absolute violence in every square centimeter of their [paintings'] surface."[18] What is true of art, is true of literature and of all speculative thinking: the immense effort to resist the given as long as the given-to can endure it, in order to phenomenalize the given. Genius only consists in a great resistance to the impact of the given. In every case, the phenomenon, which has the character of an event, takes the shape of the revealed, that is, it phenomenalizes the given-to through the same movement by which the given-to forces that which gives itself to show itself a bit more.

The revealed is neither a deep layer nor a particular region of phenomenality, but the universal mode of phenomenalization of that which gives itself in what shows itself. At the same time, it establishes the originary evential character of every phenomenon insofar as it gives itself before showing itself. The time has come, then, to raise a final question: does not the universality of the phenomenon as event, and so as a given brought to manifestation as revelation by and for a given-to, definitively abolish, de jure if not de facto, the caesura that metaphysics has unceasingly hollowed out between the world of supposedly constituted, producible, and repeatable – and thus exclusively rational – objects, on the one hand, and the world of the revealed of Revelation, the world of events neither constitutible, nor repeatable, nor immediately producible and so supposedly irrational, on the other? This caesura was imposed at the moment when the doctrine of the object attempted (and succeeded) in reducing the question and the field of phenomenality to purely apparent phenomena, deprived of the self, devalued as a being and equally as a certitude. As soon as phenomenology knew how to reopen the field of phenomenality, to include in it objects as specific cases of phenomena (impoverished and common law) and surround them with the immense region of saturated phenomena, this caesura was no longer justified. Or rather, it becomes a denial of phenomenality, itself irrational and ideological. If we admit that this caesura has no right to be, what consequences follow? That the givens retrieved by Revelation – in this instance, the unique Jewish and Christian Revelation – must be read and treated as legitimate phenomena, subject to same operations as those that result from the givens of the world: reduction to the given, eventiality, reception by the given-to, resistance, saturated phenomena, progression of the transmutation of what gives itself into what shows itself, etc. Undoubtedly, such a phenomenological place of theology necessitates (and already has) very particular protocols, conforming to the exceptional phenomena that are in question. For example, the event can have the form of a miracle, the given becomes the election and the promise, resistance of the given-to is deepened in the conversion of the witness, transmutation of what gives itself into what shows itself requires the theological virtues, its progressivity is extended in the eschatological return of the Ruler, etc. We have neither the authority nor the competence to follow up on these. But we have the right to call them to the attention of theologians. They must cease to reduce the fundamental givens of Revelation (Creation, Resurrection, miracles, divinization, etc.) to objectifying models that more or less repeat the human sciences. For the same phenomenality applies to all givens, from the most impoverished (formalisms, mathematics), to those of common law (physical sciences, technical objects), to saturated phenomena (event, idol, flesh, icon), including the possibility of phenomena that combine these four types of saturation (the phenomena of Revelation).

Translated by Beata Stawarska

Notes

*   This article has previously appeared in the *Graduate Faculty Philosophy Journal*, published by the Department of Philosophy, New School for Social Research, New York. It is reprinted here with the permission of that journal.

1. [Ed.: Here and throughout, Marion italicizes the reflexive pronoun. As he makes clear in the next paragraph, he does this to draw attention to the fact that he exploring what it means to speak of the self-givenness of the phenomenon.]

2. [Ed.: In most places "the given" translates la donation. Sometimes, however, it is translated "the donation" or "givenness."]

3. One realizes already that even the interpretation of a banal phenomenon as given not only does not prohibit hermeneutics but requires it. This is our reply to the objections of J. Grondin, in *Laval Philosophique et Théologique*, 43/44, 1987 and J. Greisch, "L'herméneutique dans la "Phénoménologie comme telle. Trois questions à propos de Réduction et donation," in *Revue de Métaphysique et de Morale*, 1991/1.

4. [Ed.: "Il nous met en scène," literally "it puts us in the (theatrical) scene."]

5. [Ed: Material in German between square brackets is in the original. Material in French was inserted by the translator or editor.]

6. I. Kant. *The Critique of Pure Reason* A163, B204.

7. We refer the reader to *Etant donné. Essai d'une phénoménologie de la donation*. Paris, 1997 and 1998, Book III, §§ 13-17.

8. Montaigne, Essais, I, 28, Oeuvres Complètes. Ed. R. Barral, Paris, 1967, p. 89.

9. E. Husserl. *On the Phenomenology of the Consciousness of Internal Time*, Hua. X, § 11, p. 29. Transl. by J. B. Brough. Kluwer Academic Publishers, 1991.

10. Ibid., § 31, p. 67.

11. Following the excellent formulation of C. Romano, *L'événement et le monde*. Paris, 1998, p. 96.

12. Descartes, *Meditationes de prima philosophia*, III, AT VII, 49, 21 sq.

13. Let it be noticed that we say "by giving a myself, a me," and not "by giving it to me," since at the moment it gives it (to me), I am precisely not there yet to receive it.

14. [Ed.: "the given-to" translates the neologism l'adonné, a past participle form.]

15. [Ed.: The French is pourpre transcendantalice, a play on words: pourpre cardinalice is an expression referring to the symbolic color associated with high church officials, as well as royalty and aristocracy.]

16. Husserl, *Ideas pertaining to a Pure Phenomenology and to a Phenomenological Philosophy. First Book.* Translated by F. Kersten. Dordrecht: Kluwer Academic Publishers, 1982. Hua. III, 140 sq.

17. [Ed.: In French, the developer, a chemical used to make the image on photographic paper visible, is called l'révélateur, "the revelator."]

18. M. Rothko, in James E. B. Breslin, *Mark Rothko. A Biography.* Chicago University Press, 1993, p. 358.

Danish Yearbook of Philosophy, Vol. *40* (2005), 79-108

DER INTENTIONALISMUS UND SEINE KRITIKER.
EIN VERMITTLUNGSVERSUCH

SØREN HARNOW KLAUSEN

University of Southern Denmark

Der Intentionalismus – auch "Repräsentationalismus" genannt – gehört zu den dominantesten Positionen in der gegenwärtigen Philosophie des Geistes. Die Theorie besagt, dass alle mentale Zustände intentional, d.h. auf einen Gegenstand gerichtet sind. Außerdem glaubt die Mehrzahl ihrer Anhänger, in der Intentionalität den Schlüssel zum Verständnis vom Bewusstsein überhaupt gefunden zu haben. Sie halten es für möglich, auf der Basis einer Theorie über mentale Repräsentation eine vollständige physikalische Erklärung des Bewusstseins zu liefern, die gleichzeitig den meisten dualistischen Intuitionen Rechnung zu tragen vermag und somit andere Spielarten des Physikalismus deutlich überlegen ist.[1]

Ich möchte mich im folgendem nicht mit dem letzten, sehr ambitiösen Vorhaben befassen. Es geht mir auch nicht hauptsächlich darum, den Intentionalismus zu verteidigen oder zu widerlegen, obgleich ich im Laufe meiner Untersuchung sowohl Lobendes als auch Kritisches über ihn sagen werde. Stattdessen möchte ich eine grundlegende Voraussetzung der ganzen gegenwärtigen Intentionalismus-Debatte in Frage stellen: Dass die "orthodoxe" Auffassung des Bewusstseins deutlich antiintentionalistisch und somit dem modernen Intentionalismus schroff entgegengesetzt sei. Denn bei näherem Hinsehen zeigt sich, dass die bekanntesten historischen Vertreter der These, es gebe auch nichtintentionale Zustände – wie etwa Husserl und Heidegger – dies nur in einem besonderen, qualifizierten Sinne gemeint haben und daher vom heutigen Intentionalismus gar nicht so weit entfernt sind. Umgekehrt deutet einiges darauf hin, dass der vermeintliche Urheber des Intentionalismus – Franz Brentano – nicht als vorbehaltloser Vertreter dieser Position gelten kann. Und diese Feststellungen sind wohlgemerkt nicht nur – und nicht primär – von historischem Interesse. Sie sind vielmehr ein deutliches Indiz dafür, dass der Intentionalismus keine Position ist, der man einfach zustimmen oder die man ablehnen sollte. Sie verlangt nach weiteren Differenzierungen, die interessanterweise auch – mehr oder weniger stillschweigend – von ihren Anhängern vorgenommen werden und den Ansichten ihrer Kritiker sehr entgegenzukommen

Ansichten ihrer Kritiker sehr entgegenzukommen scheinen. Es könnte mithin einen viel umfassenderen Konsens in der Bewusstseinstheorie geben, als bisher angenommen wurde.

I. Elemente des Intentionalismus

Die *Hauptthese* des Intentionalismus ist die obengenannte:

> (H) Alle mentale Zustände seien intentional.

Sie wird aber in der Regel zusammen mit einer Reihe von schwächeren oder stärkeren Thesen verteidigt und nicht selten mit ihnen vermengt. Eine solche ist die folgende, die ich als die intentionalistische *Kernthese* (K) bezeichnen möchte. Sie besagt, ein Unterschied im phänomenalen Charakter eines Erlebnisses spiegele sich notwendig in seinem intentionalen Gehalt wider:

> (K) Es kann keine zwei Zustände mit unterschiedlichen phänomenalen Gehalt geben, die denselben intentionalen Gehalt haben.

Anders gesagt: Es kann keine Veränderung im phänomenalen Charakter eines mentalen Zustandes geben, ohne dass der intentionale Gehalt dieses Zustandes sich entsprechend ändert.[2]

Aus K folgt, dass es so etwas wie *Qualia* nicht geben kann: qualitative Aspekte eines mentalen Zustandes, die völlig unabhängig von seinem Gehalt sind und sich daher frei variieren lassen, ohne den letzteren zu beeinflussen. K ist also keineswegs trivial. Sie wird auch von mehreren namhaften Philosophen – wie etwa Ned Block und Christopher Peacocke – bestritten.[3] Dennoch wäre es sicherlich übertrieben, sie als besonders provozierend oder geradezu revolutionär zu bezeichnen. Für einen Anhänger einer klassischen, mehr oder weniger "cartesianischen" Bewusstseinstheorie dürfte sie jedenfalls kein Stein des Anstoßes sein. Und selbst die zeitgenössischen "Freunde von Qualia" messen ihr anscheinend keine allzu große Bedeutung bei.[4]

So sollte K erstens nicht mit der folgenden, sehr populären These gleichgesetzt werden, die nur eine ihrer möglichen Deutungen ist:

> (K1) Der phänomenale Charakter wird vom intentionalen Gehalt bestimmt (er *superveniert* auf dem Gehalt).

Denn K könnte genauso sehr umgekehrt interpretiert werden, d.h. als die These, dass der Gehalt vom *phänomenalen Charakter* bestimmt wird. Die Art von Supervenienz, von der hier die Rede ist, könnte sehr wohl *symmetrisch* sein. Die folgende Deutung ist also auch legitim:

> (K2) Der intentionale Gehalt wird vom phänomenalen Charakter bestimmt (er *superveniert* auf dem phänomenalen Charakter).

Auf jeden Fall lässt K es völlig offen, welcher von den zwei Faktoren der bestimmende ist. Sie stellt nur eine gewisse Korrelation dar. Wie man das Verhältnis genauer interpretiert, wird davon abhängen, welchen Faktor man aus anderen Gründen für ontologisch fundamental hält.

Daher werde ich mir im folgenden erlauben, K so auszulegen, dass sie eine Abhängigkeit der Intentionalität vom phänomenalen Charakter impliziert. Die heutigen Intentionalisten neigen ohnehin dazu, Gehalt und phänomenalen Charakter für mehr oder weniger identisch zu halten. Und bei ihrem Versuch, den Intentionalismus zu motivieren, argumentieren sie zunächst aus der Perspektive des phänomenalen Bewusstseins. Es ist sozusagen die Intentionalität des Phänomenalen und nicht die Phänomenalität des Intentionalen, die sie zuerst aufzeigen müssen.[5]

Zweitens darf man nicht übersehen, dass K mit H zwar im Einklang ist, sie aber keineswegs impliziert. Sie besagt, dass der phänomenale Charakter eines mentalen Zustandes von seinem intentionalen Gehalt abhängt, *sofern er überhaupt einen solchen hat*; nicht aber, dass jeder mentale Zustand notwendig intentional ist. Sie schließt nicht aus, dass es mentale Zustände geben kann, denen irgendein anderer für die Intentionalität notwendiger Faktor fehlt. Es ist eines zu meinen, der phänomenale Charakter sei für den Gegenstandsbezug *mitbestimmend*, und etwas ganz anderes zu behaupten, er sei dafür allein verantwortlich. Ein Vertreter der klassischen Position würde nur die letztere, viel stärkere Behauptung bezweifeln und K dafür mehr oder weniger vorbehaltlos zustimmen.

Aus dieser Überlegung geht hervor, dass auch K2 kein adäquater Ausdruck der klassischen Auffassung sein kann. Wenn man die sehr plausible Annahme macht, alle mentalen Zustände seien *entweder* phänomenal *oder* intentional, dann folgt H tatsächlich aus K2. Denn K2 impliziert ja, dass es bei jedem Vorliegen von phänomenalen Bewusstsein auch Intentionalität geben muss. Die klassische Position ließe sich eher wie folgt ausdrücken:

(K3) Der intentionale Gehalt wird vom phänomenalen Charakter notwendig *mitbestimmt* (er superveniert auf dem phänomenalen Charakter *zusammen* mit weiteren Faktoren).

Wir werden gleich sehen, dass dies tatsächlich der Position einiger einflussreichen Philosophen entspricht.

2. Antiintentionalismus: Ein Beispiel

Nehmen wir als – nicht ganz zufällig gewähltes – Beispiel Husserl, der sowohl den Begriff der Intentionalität als auch den Antiintentionalismus nachhaltig geprägt hat. Im Gegensatz zu seinem Lehrer Brentano hat er bekanntlich die Ansicht vertreten, dass sowohl Empfindungen als auch manche Gefühle nicht zu den intentionalen Erlebnissen gehören.[6] Aber wie hat er das gemeint? Auf jeden Fall nicht so, dass man ihm die Annahme von Qualia im obengenannten Sinn zuschreiben kann. Denn er ist offensichtlich nicht der Meinung gewesen, es gebe zwei ganz verschiedene und von einander unabhängige Komponenten des Mentalen – intentionale und nicht-intentionale Erlebnisse – die zwar gemeinsam auftreten, aber einander nicht wesentlich beeinflussen.[7] Er hat der Intentionalität eine Vorrangsstellung gegeben, sie aber weiter zu analysieren versucht, und ist dabei auf Komponenten dieses komplexen Phänomens gestoßen, die nicht *für sich genommen* intentional sind. So hat Husserl die Meinung vertreten, dass die Empfindungen einen *Teil* des gesamten intentionalen Gehalt eines mentalen Aktes ausmachen und somit für die gegenständliche Beziehung des Aktes mitbestimmend sind. Er spricht z.B. davon, dass die "immanenten Charaktere" eines Erlebnisses Inhalte sind, die als *Bausteine* eines intentionalen Aktes fungieren können[8] und bezeichnet die Empfindungen als *Fundamente* der intentionalen Akte[9] sowie als "darstellende Inhalte" von Wahrnehmungen.[10]

Diese Auffassung ist, wie es von den modernen Intentionalisten hervorgehoben wird, intuitiv korrekt: Ändert sich ein qualitatives Moment einer Wahrnehmung – wie etwa eine Farbempfindung – dann ändert sich der intentionale Gegenstand entsprechend. Ich sehe z.B. nicht mehr einen braunen, sondern einen rosaroten Tisch. Die qualitativen Momente sind daher nicht intentional impotent oder indifferent.

Selbst wenn es um "primitive" Gefühle wie Schmerzempfindungen geht, kommt Husserl der intentionalistischen Auffassung entgegen:

> In gewisser Weise wird nun freilich jedes sinnliche Gefühl, z.B. der Schmerz des sich Brennens und Gebranntwerdens, auf Gegenständliches bezogen; einerseits ... auf das gebrannte Leibesglied, andererseits auf das brennende Objekt.[11]

Dies nimmt den Vorschlag moderner Intentionalisten wie Michael Tye oder Tim Crane deutlich vorweg, die Intentionalität von Schmerzen bestehe darin, einen beschädigten Körperteil als solches darzustellen oder wenigstens den Eindruck einer gewissen körperlichen *Lokalisierung* zu vermitteln.[12]

Aber warum hat Husserl dann die Empfindungen als nichtintentional bezeichnet? Weil sie eben nur *Momente* des gesamten intentionalen Zustand sind und als solche keinen *eigenen* Gegenstandsbezug haben. Sie vermitteln diesen Bezug; sie gehören sozusagen zum mentalen Mechanismus, durch den die Intentionalität zustande kommt. Und sie müssen, um bei dem Gegenstandsbezug überhaupt eine Rolle zu spielen, in einem intentionalen Kontext auftreten oder, wie Husserl sagt, sie müssen *aufgefasst* werden.[13] Der Gegenstandsbezug wird erst dadurch hergestellt, dass die Empfindungen in einer bestimmten Weise miteinander verknüpft und dadurch zu Teilen eines umfassenderen Gebildes gemacht werden.[14] Husserl weist darauf hin, zwei Zustände könnten denselben phänomenalen Charakter (d.h. denselben *Empfindungsinhalt*) und doch einen unterschiedlichen intentionalen Gehalt haben.[15] Gute Beispiele dafür sind das Betrachten von Vexierbildern und andere Arten von *Gestalt-switching*: das gleiche Empfindungsmaterial lässt unterschiedliche Auffassungen zu und begründet somit das Sehen von verschiedenen Objekten.

Diese Theorie steht offensichtlich mit K im Einklang. Sie mag mit der folgenden *starken* Variante von H unverträglich sein:

> (H1) Alle mentalen Zustände sind *notwendig* – und *durchaus* – intentional,

der zufolge das Wesen des Mentalen sich also gleichsam in die Intentionalität erschöpft. Aber eine schwächere Variante, die nur besagt, dass jeder Zustand ein intentionales *Potential* oder *Wert* haben, stimmt mit der traditionellen Konzeption sehr wohl überein:

> (H2) Alle mentalen Zustände haben einen intentionalen Wert. Ein primitiver phänomenaler Zustand liefert einen Beitrag zum intentionalen Gehalt eines komplexen mentalen Zustands, wenn er Teil eines solchen ist.

Es lässt sich freilich nicht bestreiten, dass manche Äußerungen Husserls auch K zu widersprechen scheinen. Er weist z.b. darauf hin, dass wir "im Wechsel der erlebten Inhalte einen und denselben Gegenstand zu erfassen vermeinen".[16] Dabei denkt er an das Phänomen der *Objektpermanenz*: unsere Empfindungen wechseln ständig, aber wir vermögen trotzdem Objekte als solche wahrzunehmen und gleichsam über den Wandel der Empfindungen hinwegzusehen. Wenn ich z.b. einen Fußballspieler auf dem Spielfeld betrachte, nehme ich ihn kontinuierlich als dieselbe Person wahr, obwohl er mir in einer Vielzahl von visuellen "Abschattungen" gegeben ist. Widerspricht die Anerkennung dieses sehr verbreiteten Phänomens nicht K? Impliziert die Objektpermanenz nicht, dass Unterschiede im phänomenalen Charakter der Wahrnehmungen manchmal keinen Einfluss auf ihren intentionalen Gehalt haben?

Dies wäre meiner Ansicht nach eine überspitzte Konklusion. Es mag zwar stimmen, dass wir ein solches "Identitätsbewusstsein" und unsere Wahrnehmungen daher einen *in gewisser Hinsicht* unveränderten intentionalen Inhalt haben. Auf jeden Fall scheint es berechtigt zu sagen, dass der Gegenstand *derselbe* bleibt. Aber der intentionale Gehalt eines mentalen Zustands ist mit seinem Gegenstand nicht schlechthin identisch. Der Gegenstand ist immer unter einem bestimmten Aspekt gegeben. Und dieser Aspekt ist es, der den Gehalt des Aktes ausmacht.[17] Deswegen muss sich einer Veränderung in der Weise, wie ein Objekt erscheint, notwendig in dem Gehalt der Wahrnehmung widerspiegeln. Das Phänomen der Objektpermanenz gibt also keinen Grund zur Annahme eines schlichten, statischen Identitätsbewusstsein. Es handelt sich vielmehr um das Erleben einer Identität "in der Mannigfaltigkeit". Ich nehme den Fußballspieler als *sich in bestimmter Weise bewegend* wahr. Hätte ich andere visuellen Empfindungen gehabt, hätte ich ihn nicht als sich in dieser Weise bewegend wahrgenommen.

So ist das Phänomen der Objektpermanenz ein weiterer Beleg für die These, zur Intentionalität im prägnanten Sinne gehöre *mehr* als nur ein Empfindungsinhalt. Es scheint sogar K zu unterstützen. Denn wenn der Gehalt meiner Wahrnehmung unverändert bliebe, würde man wohl kaum von einem besonderen, psychologisch und philosophisch interessanten Phänomen reden. Dass mir beim Nachdenken über ein mathematisches Problem die Zahl π stets als derselbe Gegenstand gegeben ist, kann nicht als ein Fall von Objektpermanenz gelten. Diese Identität ja nicht ähnlich komplex und problematisch. Der mathematische Denkakt vermittelt keinen Eindruck von einem Gegenstand, der sich wandelt oder von verschiedenen räumlichen Perspektiven aus wahrgenommen wird. Die Wahrnehmung dagegen lässt den Gegenstand als *denselben* erscheinen, ohne dass er jedoch phänomenologisch – oder anders gesagt, als volles intentionales Objekt betrachtet – völlig *gleich* bleibt.

3. Phänomenales Bewusstsein ohne Intentionalität?

Ein weiterer Grund, warum die Traditionalisten H nicht vorbehaltlos akzeptieren können, ist der folgende: Es scheint mindestens denkbar, dass es andere, primitivere Lebewesen geben könnte, die ein rein phänomenales Bewusstsein haben. Sie würden nur "dumpfe" Gefühle von Hunger, Schmerz oder Lust spüren, diese aber nicht als Repräsentationen von Gegenständen oder Sachverhalten auffassen.[18] Frege hat in seinem späten Aufsatz "Der Gedanke" eine ähnliche Vermutung aufgestellt:

> Sinneseindrücke ... allein öffnen uns nicht die Außenwelt. Vielleicht gibt es ein Wesen, dass nur Sinneseindrücke hat ohne Dinge zu sehen oder zu tasten. Das Haben von Sinneseindrücken ist noch kein Sehen von Dingen ... Das Haben von Gesichtseindrücken ist zwar nötig zum Sehen der Dinge, aber nicht hinreichend.[19]

Frege ist offensichtlich mit K einverstanden. Er bemerkt z.B., dass es *unter anderem* an den Gesichtseindrücken liegt, dass man ein bestimmtes Objekt als solches wahrnimmt. Dafür lehnt er H entschieden ab: Um ein Objekt wahrzunehmen, bedarf es etwas Zusätzlichem, das er als *nichtsinnlich* bezeichnet. Diese zusätzliche Komponente fasst Frege allerdings in einer ausgeprägt rationalistischen (oder kantischen) Weise auf, die nicht für die orthodoxe Position im Allgemeinen kennzeichnend ist: als *begrifflich* und möglicherweise sogar als *propositional*.[20] Es ist klar, dass eine solche Auffassung antiintentionalistisch ist. Aber eine moderatere, weniger rationalistische Variante derselben Grundansicht – wie die von Husserl vertretene – ist dem Intentionalismus weniger schroff entgegengesetzt. Die Anhänger der traditionellen Konzeption stimmen in der Regel mit den modernen Intentionalisten in der Annahme überein, nicht nur Bewusstsein, sondern auch Intentionalität sei ein primitives Phänomen, das unabhängig von höheren kognitiven Fähigkeiten vorkommen kann. Sie teilen z.B. die Ansicht Dretskes, es gebe ein "einfaches Sehen", das weder propositional noch begrifflich sei.[21] Und sie würden Dretske und Tye darin recht geben, dass phänomenale Zustände nicht von mentalen Zuständen höherer Ordnung – wie Aufmerksamkeit, Reflexion oder Begreifen – abhängig sind (die letztere These würde Frege auch akzeptieren).

Die Vertreter der klassischen Position würden diese Annahme mit denselben Argumenten verteidigen, die von den modernen Intentionalisten vorgebracht wurden:[22] dass wir viel reichhaltigere und "feinkörnigere" Erfahrungen haben, als wir imstande sind begrifflich zu fassen; dass wir häufig im Nachhinein feststellen können, etwas wahrgenommen zu haben, das wir aber im Hitze des Gefechtes nicht unmittelbar *bemerkt*, geschweige denn zum Thema eines expliziten Urteils gemacht haben (z.b. eine Wandfarbe oder ein Kleidungsstück eines Gesprächspartners); und dass derselbe Wahrnehmungsinhalt in verschiedener Weise konzeptualisiert oder in verschiedenen Propositionen ausgedrückt werden kann (z.b. "Sie sitzt auf dem Stuhl" und "der Stuhl trägt sie").[23]

Immerhin werden die meisten Traditionalisten darauf beharren, dass selbst in Fällen von einfacher, nichtbegrifflicher Wahrnehmung eine gewisse integrative oder "synthetisierende" Leistung vollzogen werden muss und dass dies die zusätzliche Bedingung neben den Empfindungsinhalten ausmacht. Sie platzieren sich somit zwischen der Kant-Frege Position, der zufolge ein begriffliches oder propositionales Element hinzukommen muss, und der empiristisch geprägten Auffassung vieler zeitgenössischen Intentionalisten, dass das Haben von Empfindungen für die Intentionalität *hinreichend* sei.[24] Sie sind der Meinung, dass es im Gehalt einer Wahrnehmung Elemente gibt, die nicht zu den Empfindungsinhalten im engeren Sinne gehören, aber dennoch vor jeder Konzeptualisierung *gegeben* sind (wie z.b. Strukturmomente oder Gestaltqualitäten).[25]

Bleiben wir aber zunächst bei der Behauptung, dass es Formen des nichtintentionalen Bewusstsein geben kann. Wie soll man sich das genauer vorstellen? Schmerzen sind zugegebenermaßen häufig intentional und es stimmt vermutlich auch, dass sie in der Regel Verletzungen von bestimmten Körperteilen repräsentieren. Nach der traditionellen Auffassung ist diese Intentionalität jedoch kein intrinsisches Merkmal der Schmerzen. Sie erfüllen im Normalfall diese Funktion, d.h. sie bilden die Grundlage des betreffenden intentionalen Aktes, indem sie auf ein verletztes Körperteil bezogen werden. Aber es bleibt zumindest denkbar, dass sie unabhängig von dieser – und jeder anderen – repräsentativen Funktion auftreten könnten. Wäre es z.b. nicht möglich, dass einem Organismus die Proprioception fehlt, so dass er gar nicht imstande ist, die Teile seines eigenen Körpers zu lokalisieren? Manche Philosophen behaupten zwar, dass es ohne Proprioception oder andere Formen von körperlicher Selbstwahrnehmung gar kein Selbstbewusstsein geben kann.[26] Aber man braucht auch nicht anzunehmen, dass der Organismus Selbstbewusstsein in diesem Sinne – die Fähigkeit, sich selbst mentale Zustände *zuzuschreiben* – besitzt. Es genügt, dass er die Schmerzempfindungen einfach *hat*, d.h. sich in ihnen *befindet* (außerdem ließe sich dafür argumentieren, dass ein solches "haben" von Empfindungen mit einer noch rudimentäreren Form des Selbstbewusstseins – einem Selbstbewusstsein, das die Fähigkeit der Selbstzuschreibung nicht einschließt – verbunden ist).[27]

Diese Hypothese wird von der Vermutung unterstützt, man könne in einem gewissen Sinne *denselben* Schmerz in einem Finger wie in einem Zeh haben. Auf jeden Fall kann man wohl denselben Schmerz in seinem linken wie in seinem rechten Bein spüren. Und wenn dies so ist, kann es nur ein kontingenter Sachverhalt sein, dass etwa Finger- und Zehschmerzen qualitativ verschieden sind. Die Hypothese der Trennbarkeit von Schmerzempfindung *an sich* und dem intentionalen Gehalt des Schmerzzustandes wird auch von den Berichten über nichtlokalisierbaren Schmerzen bestätigt (die z.B. durch Elektrotortur verursacht werden).

Nun könnte es aber aussehen, als ob die Hypothese der Trennbarkeit nicht nur H, sondern auch K widerspricht. Ned Block interpretiert sie angeblich in dieser Weise. Er hält es für möglich, dass zwei Schmerzzustände in Bezug auf alle repräsentationsrelevante Eigenschaften identisch und trotzdem qualitativ verschieden sein können.[28] Ob und inwiefern man Block in dieser Vermutung folgen mag, hängt jedoch – wie vieles in der Intentionalismus-Debatte – davon ab, wie weit man den Begriff des intentionalen Gehalts (oder des intentionalen Objektes) fasst. Ich würde das von Block erwähnte Beispiel – es sei möglich, dass zwei verschiedene Schmerzen in allen Aspekten identisch sind, die durch unsere Sprache erfasst werden können (Intensität, Lokalisierung usw.) – analog zum Phänomen der Objektpermanenz deuten: ja, es ist möglich, dass der intentionale Gegenstand eines Schmerzzustandes *derselbe* bleibt, obwohl der qualitative Charakter der Schmerzempfindung sich verändert. Aber die Veränderung der Qualität bewirkt nichtsdestotrotz eine Veränderung in der Weise, *wie* der intentionale Gegenstand sich darstellt (als stechend, brennend oder womöglich auch so, dass wir über keine adäquate Beschreibung verfügen. Es gibt keinen Grund anzunehmen, dass alle Aspekte des intentionalen Gehalts mittels der vorhandenen Sprache erfasst werden können). Also bleibt der *volle* intentionale Gehalt der Schmerzzustände nicht unverändert und K behält seine Gültigkeit. Die Schmerzempfindung liefert einen Beitrag zum intentionalen Gehalt und ist somit für den Gegenstandsbezug mitbestimmend – aber sie ist nicht dafür *hinreichend*.

4. Intentionalität im weiteren Sinne

Was könnte der Intentionalist – d.h. ein Vertreter von H1 – zur Möglichkeit eines rein spürenden, animalischen, nichtintentionalen Bewusstsein sagen? Vermutlich würde er einwenden, dass die Erlebniszustände eines jeden Organismus, seien sie auch noch so primitiv, doch einen gewissen intentionalen Gehalt haben müssen. Immerhin ist alles Bewusstsein ja Bewusstsein *von* etwas: etwas erscheint dem Organismus – es ist ihm in irgendeiner besonderen Weise "zumute" oder er ist mit irgendeinem phänomenalen Vorgang oder Zustand unmittelbar bekannt.

Dies lässt sich kaum bestreiten. Phänomenales Bewusstsein impliziert, dass *etwas jemandem erscheint*, und zwar in bestimmter Weise. Umgekehrt darf nicht übersehen werden, dass es sich hier um eine deutlich andere Art von Gegenstandsbezug als im Falle einer Wahrnehmung oder eines Denkaktes handelt. Der Begriff des intentionalen Gehalts wird so weit gedehnt, dass der Intentionalismus beinahe trivial gemacht wird. Er wird gleichsam auf die These reduziert, Bewusstsein besitze immer eine gewisse interne Komplexität und lasse sich in verschiedene Komponenten zerlegen.[29] Sicherlich ist es nicht falsch zu sagen, dass selbst ein sehr primitiver Organismus seinen Schmerz als einen solchen erleben muss, und dass dieses Erlebnis in gewisser Weise eine dyadische Struktur besitzt. Wenn man aber diese *immanente* und sehr rudimentäre Polarität bereits als eine Manifestation von Intentionalität versteht, dann werden selbst hartgesottene Antiintentionalisten zugeben, dass alle Bewusstseinszustände *in diesem Sinne* intentional sind.[30]

Gerade solch ein umfassender Begriff von Intentionalität ist es aber, der Franz Brentanos angeblichem "Intentionalismus" zugrunde liegt. Brentano hat bekanntlich die These aufgestellt, das Wesensmerkmal der Bewusstseinszustände sei die Intentionalität, d.h. die "Richtung auf ein Objekt" oder die "Beziehung auf einen Inhalt".[31] Damit hat er jedoch nicht mehr gemeint, als dass dem Bewusstsein *etwas gegeben* sein muss. Dies lässt sich in verschiedener Weise belegen. Zum einen muss darauf hingewiesen werden, dass Brentano den Begriff "Vorstellung" (der dem modernen Begriff der Repräsentation entspricht) in einem sehr weiten Sinne verwendet. "Vorgestellt werden" bedeutet für ihn so viel wie "erscheinen".[32] Und bereits seine Rede von der "intentionalen Inexistenz" des Gegenstandes[33] deutet an, dass es sich um keinen Gegenstandsbezug im robusten externalistischen Sinne handelt. Intentionalität schließt nach seiner Auffassung nicht ein, dass ein Erlebnis mit irgendeinem anderen Phänomen in Verbindung steht – und erst gar nicht, dass es von physischen Dingen oder Eigenschaften verursacht wird. Die letzteren spielen überhaupt keine Rolle in Brentanos Bewusstseinstheorie.[34]

Freilich wird von den modernen Intentionalisten ebenfalls behauptet, ein mentaler Zustand könne einen intentionalen Gehalt haben, ohne dass sein Gegenstand wirklich existiere.[35] Die Rede vom intentionalen Gehalt ist gerade durch die Einsicht motiviert, dass ein Erlebnis "von" etwas sein kann, das gar nicht wirklich ist, aber nur gehofft, geträumt oder vorgestellt wird. Dennoch bleibt ein wichtiger Unterschied zwischen Brentano und den meisten zeitgenössischen Intentionalisten. Denn sie räumen dem intentionalen Gehalt nur eine beschränkte Autonomie ein; schließlich wollen sie ihn ja auf objektive, physikalische Relationen reduzieren. Ein mentaler Zustand kann nach der Ansicht von Tye zwar intentional sein, obwohl sein Objekt nicht existiert; seine Intentionalität verdankt er jedoch dem Umstand, dass er unter optimalen Umständen mit seinem Gegenstand *kausal kovariiert*.[36] Dretske ergänzt diese Erklärung mit der Annahme, die Intentionalität habe eine natürliche, evolutionär festgelegte Funktion.[37] Tye und Dretske postulieren somit eine *generelle* Abhängigkeit der Intentionalität von der objektiven Beschaffenheit der Welt. Der Gehalt setzt die Existenz des entsprechenden partikulären Gegenstandes nicht voraus, aber er wird trotzdem durch extramentale Sachverhalte konstituiert.

Überhaupt tendieren die zeitgenössischen Intentionalisten dazu, die Intentionalität und damit das Bewusstsein von weiteren Faktoren abhängig zu machen. So betont Tye zwar wiederholt, dass phänomenales Bewusstsein nicht mit Urteilen, Glauben oder irgendwelchen anderen "höheren" Bewusstseins-zuständen vermengt werden darf.[38] Aber letztendlich spricht er einem Wesen, das keine *beliefs* und *desires* haben kann, den Besitz eines phänomenalen Bewusstsein kategorisch ab.[39] Und an einer anderen Stelle rechnet er die Fähigkeiten des *Räsonierens* und der *Verhaltensänderung* zu Grundbedingungen des phänomenalen Bewusstseins.[40]

Dagegen ist es für Brentanos Version des Intentionalismus charakteristisch, dass die Intentionalität als eine *intrinsische* Eigenschaft des Bewusstseins verstanden wird. Das psychische Phänomen *enthält* etwas als Objekt *in sich*. Diese "immanente Gegenständlichkeit" [41] wird für eine nicht weiter erklärbare Grundtatsache gehalten. Außerdem verlangt Brentano nicht einmal, dass ein intentionaler Zustand einen *vermeintlich* physischen Gegenstand haben muss. Er ist z.b. nicht der Ansicht, dass Schmerzen immer Körperzustände repräsentieren, sondern meint nur, dass sie einen besonderen Empfindungs-inhalt haben und dass das Schmerzempfinden daher eine dyadische Struktur, eine gewisse "Zweiheit in der Einheit", [42] besitzt. Und er stimmt sogar der Ansicht zu, primitive Gefühle hätten gewissermaßen nur *sich selbst* als Objekt[43] – eine Pointe, die später von Searle als Argument *gegen* den Intentionalismus vorgebracht worden ist.[44]

Insgesamt zeigt Brentanos Diskussion mit den Antiintentionalisten seiner Zeit – vor allem mit Hamilton[45] – dass er nicht die Grundzüge ihrer Phänomenbeschreibung in Frage stellt, sondern nur darauf beharrt, dass die betreffende Phänomene als Fälle von Intentionalität zu bezeichnen sind. Es wäre sicherlich übertrieben, diese Frage für rein terminologisch zu halten. Aber es wäre nicht weniger falsch zu behaupten, es handele sich um einen Zusammenprall zweier völlig verschiedener Auffassungen des Mentalen. Die Diskussion zwischen Intentionalisten und Antiintentionalisten scheint eine Familienangelegenheit zu sein, solange man sich auf die Kern- und Haupt-thesen konzentriert und von den reduktionistischen Hintergedanken absieht, mit denen der Intentionalismus heute ins Feld geführt wird.

5. Externalistischer Intentionalismus

Wie anfangs gesagt, ist es nicht meine Absicht, den Intentionalismus grund-sätzlich zu kritisieren. Dennoch möchte ich auf einige Umstände aufmerksam machen, die ihn vielleicht etwas weniger vorteilhaft erscheinen lassen. Erstens muss hervorgehoben werden, dass es nur die sehr liberale – brentanosche – Variante der Theorie ist, die beanspruchen kann, intuitiv plausibel und phänomenologisch begründet zu sein. Vieles spricht dafür, dass alle mentale Zustände intentional sind in einem weiten, relativ unverpflichtenden Sinne – d.h. dass sie einen bestimmten Charakter haben und einen entsprechen Beitrag zum intentionalen Gehalt des gesamten mentalen Zustands liefern (K3 und H2). Die weitergehende Behauptung, die für die modernen reduktionistischen Spielarten des Intentionalismus charakteristisch ist, der Gehalt aller mentaler Zustände hinge mehr oder weniger direkt von objektiven, extramentalen

Gegenständen oder Eigenschaften ab, mag auch korrekt sein. Aber sie ist eine zusätzliche Annahme und wird nicht von der Analyse des Bewusstseins direkt unterstützt.

Dies mag zunächst nicht besonders problematisch erscheinen. Einen Physikalisten wird es kaum überraschen, dass die Natur der Repräsentation nicht allein durch phänomenologische Beschreibung oder Begriffsanalyse festgelegt werden kann. Er wird zugeben, dass seine Version des Intentionalismus eine weitere Begründung braucht, weil er davon überzeugt ist, eine solche liefern zu können. Die brentanosche "Minimaltheorie" hält er für unzulänglich, da sie die Repräsentation nur von innen untersucht und das zentrale Problem des Bezugs zur realen Welt ausklammert. Außerdem findet er die Rede von Intentionalität als intrinsische Eigenschaft mysteriös und unwissenschaftlich. Sie scheint ihm etwas zu sein, was nach einer weiteren Erklärung verlangt. Aber zum Glück gibt es heute eine Reihe von vielversprechenden naturalistischen Repräsentationstheorien, mithilfe deren eine solche Erklärung gegeben werden kann. So besteht die Strategie des modernen reduktionistischen Intentionalisten (den ich im folgenden als E-Intentionalisten bezeichnen werde, weil er in der Regel von einer *externalistischen* Theorie des Intionalität gebrauch macht)[46] darin, H erst durch phänomenologische Analysen plausibel zu machen und dann anschließend der intentionale Gehalt, der in dieser Weise im Bewusstsein gleichsam aufgefunden wurde, durch unabhängige, aber bewährte und sachlich relevante Theorien weiter zu bestimmen.

Dies ist jedoch leichter gesagt als getan. Es scheint auf dem ersten Blick, als würde der Intentionalismus zum Physikalismus besonders gut passen, weil er das Bewusstsein gleichsam aus dem Kopf – und aus dem seelischen Innenleben – verstößt und mit der Außenwelt in Verbindung bringt. Aber er ist ein zweischneidiges Schwert. Zwar macht er das Bewusstsein von dessen Gegenstand abhängig. Aber der Gegenstand wird dadurch auch als Gegenstand des *Bewusstseins* – und wohlgemerkt des *phänomenalen* Bewusstseins – aufgefasst (vgl. auch die anfangs gemachte Beobachtung, die Abhängigkeitsbeziehung sei mehr oder weniger symmetrisch). Das spricht zunächst für die brentanosche Minimaltheorie: Der intentionale Gegenstand ist einfach das, was dem Subjekt erscheint.[47] Er wird vom phänomenalen Charakter des betreffenden mentalen Zustandes bestimmt und alle weitere Faktoren sind, obwohl sie für das Erlebnis kausal verantwortlich und somit für seine vollständige Erklärung durchaus relevant sein mögen, für seinen Gehalt nicht direkt *konstitutiv*. Wäre es in irgendeiner anderen Weise entstanden oder hätte es andere oder gar keine Relationen zur Außenwelt gehabt, würde es trotzdem denselben Gehalt haben.

Diese Pointe lässt sich präziser formulieren. Die E-Intentionalisten übersehen häufig, dass der Intentionalismus an sich keineswegs einen semantischen Externalismus impliziert. H sagt nichts darüber, wie der intentionale Gehalt genauer zu verstehen ist. Und die Verfechter der traditionellen Bewusstseinstheorie haben alle den Externalismus abgelehnt – dies gilt, wie ich gerade gezeigt habe, auch für Brentano. Ein internalistischer Intentionalismus treibt aber das Projekt einer physikalistischen Reduktion des Bewusstseins kaum voran (auch wenn er ihm nicht gerade im Wege steht). Er verlagert lediglich das Problem auf das Gebiet der Intentionalität, die es noch zu erklären gilt.

Nun könnte man vielleicht dazu sagen, dass der Externalismus immerhin die mit Abstand plausibelste Theorie des Gehalts ist, über die wir gegenwärtig verfügen. Dass er von den älteren Philosophen nicht angenommen wurde, ist in diesem Zusammenhang irrelevant. Entscheidend ist, dass u.a. Kripke, Putnam und Burge gezeigt haben, dass er nicht nur theoretisch überlegen ist, sondern auch durch verbreitete Intuitionen unterstützt wird. Darauf läst sich jedoch erwidern, dass es hier nicht um die Frage geht, inwiefern der Externalismus allgemein dem Internalismus vorzuziehen ist, sondern wie gut er zum *Intentionalismus* passt. Nicht von ungefähr beharren viele Externalisten darauf, die Repräsentationsproblematik vom Problem des phänomenalen Bewusstsein scharf zu trennen.[48] Ihrer Ansicht nach ist der phänomenale Charakter unserer mentalen Zuständen – wenn es ihn überhaupt gibt – für ihren intentionalen Gehalt irrelevant. So gesehen teilen sie die traditionelle Auffassung des Bewusstseins, obwohl sie ganz andere Konsequenzen daraus ziehen.

Die E-Intentionalisten können aber diesen Weg nicht gehen. Ihre Hauptpointe ist ja gerade, dass der phänomenale Charakter durchaus repräsentationsrelevant ist. Das stellt sie vor das Problem, dass eine solche Auffassung sich mit einer externalistischen Gehaltstheorie – die in der Regel von den subjektiven Aspekten der Repräsentation absieht[49] – schwerlich vereinbar scheint.

Diese Schwierigkeit darf freilich nicht übertrieben werden. So kann man natürlich nicht einfach voraussetzen, dass der phänomenale Charakter ein intrinsisches Merkmal des Bewusstseins ist. Denn gerade diese Auffassung ist es ja, die von den E-Intentionalisten abgelehnt wird. Sie bemühen sich darum, den Gegensatz zwischen Internalismus und Externalismus gleichsam aufzuheben, indem der phänomenale Charakter ebenso wie der intentionale Gehalt in der Außenwelt verankert wird. Dretske bezeichnet somit seine Position als "phänomenaler Externalismus" und versucht es plausibel zu machen, dass alle unsere Erlebnisse durch ihre Beziehungen zu externen Sachverhalten individuiert werden.[50]

Dieser Weg bleibt sicherlich dem E-Intentionalisten offen. Er kann aber die Wahrheit des Externalismus wiederum auch nicht einfach voraussetzen. Es ist das theoretische "Gesamtpaket" – Intentionalismus *und* Externalismus – dessen Plausibilität es zu zeigen gilt. Und es gibt weiterhin einiges, das gegen diese Kombination spricht.

Zum Einen ist der Externalismus bezüglich des Phänomenalen nicht im gleichen Maße intuitiv wie der Externalismus bezüglich des Gehalt von Begriffen oder Meinungen. Das ist wohl auch der Grund, warum viele Externalisten den Intentionalismus ablehnen.[51] Denn im Gegensatz zu "künstlichen" oder theoretischen Entitäten wie Begriffen oder der Gehalt von Gedanken scheinen unsere Erlebnisse etwas zu sein, das einen eigenen Charakter besitzt und nicht erst durch unsere *Zuschreibungen* seine Identität verliehen bekommt. Freilich ist nach vielen externalistischen Theorien die Intentionalität eine reale Eigenschaft, die nicht zuschreibungsabhängig ist; das gilt z.B. für Dretskes Repräsentationstheorie.[52] Aber man könnte meinen, dass ein solcher Externalismus bereits etwas von seiner intuitiven Basis verloren hat. Die klassischen Argumente für den semantischen Externalismus stützen sich darauf, was wir über die Bedeutung eines Begriffes oder den Gehalt eines Glaubenszustands *sagen würden*.[53] Auch wenn sie den sozialen Charakter der Bedeutung nicht unmittelbar voraussetzen und – vor allem bei Kripke und Putnam – ein deutlich realistisches Flair haben, verweisen sie immerhin darauf, wie die Bedeutung durch eine besondere menschliche Praxis fixiert und aufrechterhalten wird. Außerdem beruht der Widerstand gegen den phänomenalen Externalismus nicht nur auf der Vermutung, dass der Charakter unserer Erlebnisse nicht *von uns* festgelegt wird, sondern auf die allgemeinere Überzeugung, dass er gar nicht relational bestimmt ist. In dieser Hinsicht wird er analog zu einer physikalischen – und nicht zu einer semantischen – Eigenschaft aufgefasst.[54]

Das sind zunächst nur Intuitionen, die nicht von allen Philosophen geteilt werden und vielleicht auch nicht ganz verlässlich sind. Aber zum Zweiten

haben externalistische Repräsentationstheorien bekanntlich damit Schwierigkeiten, die Feinkörnigkeit der Repräsentation zu erklären. Da sie versuchen,
die Intentionalität auf einen mehr oder weniger "reinen" Gegenstandbezug zu
reduzieren, sind sie tendenziell blind für diejenigen semantischen Unterschiede, die auf verschiedenen *Gegebenheitsweisen* eines Gegenstandes beru-
hen. Für die einfachsten kausalen Theorien – wie etwa die der kausalen Ko-
varianz, auf die Tye interessanterweise setzt – zeigt sich dieser Mangel an
Feinkörnigkeit bereits auf der Ebene sprachlicher Bedeutungen. Die Theorie
kann den Bedeutungsunterschied zwischen (angeblich) koextensionalen
Ausdrücken wie "Tier mit Herz" und "Tier mit Niere" kaum erklären – den
Unterschied zwischen *notwendig* koextensionalen Ausdrücken wie "Dreieck
mit drei gleichen Winkeln" und "gleichseitiges Dreieck" erst gar nicht. Denn
ein notwendiger Zusammenhang kann nicht durch einen Verweis auf
kontrafaktische Umstände aufgelöst werden. Und im Falle der Wahrnehmung
– die *ex hypothesi* noch viel feinkörniger ist – wird das Problem womöglich
noch akuter. Was ist der Unterschied zwischen dem Sehen eines roten Apfels,
dem Sehen eines besonderen Aggregats von Molekülen und dem Sehen einer
besonderen Konfiguration von gereizten Netzhautzellen? Jeder sensorische
Zustand ist mit einer ganzen Reihe von Gegenständen und Sachverhalten – mit
näheren sowohl als auch entfernteren Gliedern der Kette seiner Ursachen und
sogar mit disjunktiven Sachverhalten – gleichermaßen korreliert.[55]

Selbstverständlich haben die Externalisten vieles versucht, um diese
Probleme der semantischen Unbestimmtheit zu beheben.[56] Nur muss klar sein,
dass es dem E-Intentionalisten nicht erlaubt ist, unreduzierte intentionale
Elemente in die Theorie einzuschmuggeln, wie etwa eine subjektive Perspektive auf den – externalistisch festgelegten – Gehalt. Denn jeder Unterschied im
subjektiven Charakter muss nach dem E-Intentionalismus selbst wiederum
externalistisch erklärt werden. Bereits der scheinbar harmlose Zusatz "unter
optimalen Bedingungen", mit denen die kausalen Theorien üblicherweise
ergänzt werden,[57] mag unzulässig sein, weil er die Erklärung zirkulär macht:[58]
Wir können die optimalen Bedingungen erst dann identifizieren, wenn wir
bereits wissen, was der betreffende Zustand repräsentieren *soll* – d.h. wenn wir
seinen intentionalen Gehalt kennen. Optimal oder ideal zu sein ist offensichtlich keine fundamentale, natürliche Eigenschaft. Sie ist normativ und muss
daher selbst weiter reduzierbar sein.

Ein Verweis auf Unterschiede im "Format" oder "Modus" der Repräsentationen ist ebenfalls nicht unproblematisch. Natürlich stimmt es, dass z.B. der

Unterschied zwischen dem Sehen, dem Fühlen und des Schmecken eines Apfels auf Unterschiede im sensorischen Modus beruht. Aber dies scheint ein beachtliches Zugeständnis zu sein, das den Unterschied zwischen Intentionalismus und Antiintentionalismus nochmals verkleinert. Denn nach dieser Auffassung gibt es also doch Unterschiede im phänomenalen Charakter von Erlebnissen, deren Gegenstände sonst – objektiv gesehen – identisch sind.[59]

Die konsequenteste und vielversprechendste Strategie des E-Intentionalisten besteht wohl darin, die nötige semantische Fernkörnigkeit durch einen Rekurs auf die Evolutionsgeschichte herbeizuschaffen. Die repräsentierten Eigenschaften und Gegenstände seien diejenigen, für deren Repräsentation der betreffende kognitive Mechanismus selektiert wurde: Fliegen z.b. und nicht kleine schwarzen Flecken.[60] Es bleibt jedoch umstritten, inwiefern die semantische Unterbestimmtheit sich auf diese Weise völlig beheben lässt. Die evolutionsgeschichtliche Betrachtungsweise scheint gegenüber vielen Bedeutungsunterschieden indifferent zu sein.[61] Und es bleibt noch fragwürdiger, inwiefern die Theorie auf die Repräsentationsfunktion *phänomenaler* Zustände zutrifft.

Außerdem bekommt man leicht den Eindruck, dass die "darwinistischen" Repräsentationstheorien den intentionalen Gehalt von Faktoren abhängig machen, die schlichtweg *zu* extern und damit semantisch – oder auf jeden Fall psychologisch – irrelevant sind. Wie kann die Evolutionsgeschichte – d.h. etwas *Vergangenes* – für den phänomenalen Charakter meines aktuellen Erlebnisses konstitutiv sein? Der phänomenale Charakter von Erlebnissen scheint etwas zu sein, was in eminenter Weise durch seine *aktualen* Eigenschaften bestimmt sind.

Michael Tye sieht dies ähnlich und lehnt daher die evolutionäre Betrachtungsweise ab. Er teilt die gängige Meinung, dass zwei Organismen, die dieselben intrinsischen Eigenschaften haben und sich in derselben Umgebung befinden, sowohl phänomenal als auch intentional identisch sein müssen, auch wenn einer von ihnen spontan entstanden ist und somit gar keine evolutionäre Vorgeschichte hat.[62] Dies deutet aber darauf hin, dass Tye an der generellen Vereinbarkeit seines Intentionalismus mit dem Externalismus letzten Endes zweifelt. Die Intuitionen, auf die er sich bei seiner Ablehnung der evolutionären Betrachtungsweise beruft, sind deutlich internalistisch: Kontextuelle Faktoren seien für den Gehalt irrelevant. Dann stellt sich die Frage, warum man nicht ebenfalls die Relevanz der Beschaffenheit der *Umwelt* bestreiten sollte. Wenn ein spontan entstandener Organismus intentionale und phänomenale Zustände besitzt, warum nicht auch ein Organismus, dessen kausalen Beziehungen zur Außenwelt abnormal sind, wie etwa ein Gehirn im Tank?[63] Es darf nicht übersehen werden, dass der Gehalt nach der von Tye bevorzugte Kovariationstheorie (ein sensorischer Zustand repräsentiere P, falls er unter optimalen Bedingungen dann – und nur dann – vorkomme, wenn P, und er durch P verursacht werde)[64] durch *modale* Eigenschaften bestimmt wird. Der Zustand habe seinen besonderen Gehalt, weil er sich unter gewissen Umständen, die vielleicht nicht wirklich bestehen, so und so verhalten *würde*. Solche Eigenschaften sind gewissermaßen noch externer als die historischen, die ja immerhin *aktual* (d.h. nicht nur *möglich*) sind. Für einen Naturalisten sollte es ohnehin wichtig sein, modale Eigenschaften auf aktuale reduzieren zu können. In diesem Fall würde es aber bedeuten, dass man auf den intentionalen Gehalt des sensorischen Zustands zurückgreifen müsste, ihn also für etwas bereits Gegebenes ansähe. Das ist auch, was Tye *de facto* tut. Denn er hat offensichtlich eine genaue, aber nicht weiter erläuterte Idee von der "normalen Funktion" eines intentionalen Zustandes.[65] Diese Denkweise ist jedoch entweder zirkulär oder sie läuft auf eine internalistische Auffassung hinaus, der zufolge der Gehalt nicht durch Umweltfaktoren bestimmt wird.

Wenn Tye sein E-intentionalistisches Programm konsequent durchführen wollte, müsste er vielmehr die Verlässlichkeit der internalistischen Intuitionen – einschließlich seiner eigenen Intuitionen zugunsten spontan entstandenen Organismen – grundsätzlich in Frage stellen. Dann würde er seine Theorie jedoch viel von seiner Verträglichkeit mit der klassischen Auffassung des Bewusstseins (und mit dem *Common Sense* im Allgemeinen) einbüßen.

Bekanntermaßen ist sehr umstritten, welche Rolle Intuitionen bei der Beurteilung philosophischer Positionen spielen dürfen. Aber gleichgültig, ob man die internalistischen Intuitionen teilt oder nicht – zumindest gilt, dass der E-Intentionalist vor der Aufgabe steht, für jeden phänomenalen Charakter eine entsprechende objektive Eigenschaft zu finden. Und er kann dabei nicht auf die Möglichkeit verschiedener perspektivischer Darstellungen derselben Eigenschaft zurückgreifen, weil dieser Unterschied selbst wiederum durch Unterschiede in der objektiven Beschaffenheit des Objektes erklärt werden muss. Diese Aufgabe ist *a priori* nicht unlösbar, aber sie ist auch alles andere als leicht. Blocks Überlegung, es könne verschiedener Schmerzqualitäten bei der gleichen Körperverletzung (und des gleichen Lokalisierungs- und Intensitätsgefühls) geben, ist hier durchaus relevant, auch wenn sie K nicht umzustoßen vermag. Denn der E-Intentionalist hat eine deutlich kleinere Auswahl an potentiellen Referenten zur Verfügung. Er muss reale und nicht *nur* intentionale Unterschiede aufzeigen.

Freilich ist zu erwarten, dass für jeden phänomenalen Unterschied ein physiologischer Unterschied zu finden ist. Dies ist jedoch eine triviale Konsequenz der von beinahe allen Diskussionsteilnehmern geteilten Ansicht, dass mentale Zustände auf physikalischen Zuständen supervenieren. Der E-Intentionalist muss außerdem glaubhaft machen, dass der betreffende physiologische Faktor von dem mentalen Zustand *repräsentiert* wird – und sich wohlgemerkt in seinem *phänomenalen* Charakter widerspiegelt. Eine solche Zuordnung von Körperzuständen und Erlebnissen scheint aber in vielen Fällen *ad hoc*. Unterschiedliche Empfindungsqualitäten mögen mit unterschiedlichen Nervenbahnen, Reizmuster, Gewebeverletzungen, Muskelspannungen usw. kausal zusammenhängen, aber es kann nicht ernsthaft behauptet werden, dass diese Faktoren dem Subjekt unmittelbar gegeben sind.

So behauptet Tye z.B., dass ein Orgasmus ein Erlebnis von physischen Veränderungen in den Genitalien sei. Und er kann natürlich Fälle von Orgasmus, die ohne eine tatsächliche Einwirkung auf die Genitalien vorkommen, analog zu den Phantomschmerzen erklären: Der Zustand hat den betreffenden Gehalt, weil er *unter optimalen Bedingungen* eine Veränderung in den Genitalien repräsentieren *würde*. Aber stimmt es, dass es sich bei einem Orgasmus immer so anfühlt, *als ob* die Genitalien stimuliert würden? Und wie ist es etwa mit dem Lustgefühl eines Masochisten, der sich peitschen lässt? Tye hat sicherlich recht, wenn er behauptet, der Schmerz des Masochisten habe denselben phänomenalen Charakter wie der des Nicht-Masochisten.[66] Aber der Unterschied lässt sich nicht auf verschiedene propositionale Einstellungen – wie z.B. verschiedene Bewertungen – reduzieren. Tye beschreibt ihn selbst völlig zurecht als *phänomenal*. Dann müsste er aber auch eine objektiven Eigenschaft des Repräsentierten widerspiegeln. Die Lust kann jedoch schwerlich eine weitere Repräsentation der durch das Peitschen verursachten Körperverletzung sein. Da es sich um ein sexuelles Erlebnis handelt, müsste es wohl – nach der Theorie von Tye – in den Genitalien (oder zumindest in einem sonstigen Körperteil) lokalisiert sein. Das klingt jedoch auch nicht besonders plausibel. Bei Empfindungsqualitäten wie Orgasmus oder besonders feinkörnige "Schmerzschattierungen" handelt es sich wohl eher um elementare "Gegebenheitsweisen", die zwar den intentionalen Gehalt des gesamten Erlebnisses verändern – das Peitschen wird nicht nur als schmerzhaft, sondern auch

als lusterregend empfunden – dem Subjekt aber trotzdem nicht mit physiologischen Eigenschaften als solche bekannt machen.

Der E-Intentionalismus wird also mit beachtlichen Schwierigkeiten kon-
frontiert. Ich möchte aber nochmals betonen, dass meine Überlegungen nicht
als eine grundsätzliche Kritik des Intentionalismus – auch nicht des E-
Intentionalismus – gemeint sind. Fast alle interessanten philosophischen
Theorien stellen sich als problematisch heraus, wenn man sie nach ihren
weiteren Implikationen befragt. Mit meinem Verweis auf die obengenannte
Schwierigkeiten wollte ich nur zeigen, dass der E-Intentionalismus mit ganz
anderen Problemen zu kämpfen hat als der Intentionalismus an sich – d.h. K
und H ohne weitere reduktionistische Begleitthesen. So gesehen ist er eher als
ein Argument *für* den Intentionalismus zu verstehen: Man kann die Theorie
annehmen, ohne E-Intentionalist zu sein. Die Stellungnahme zu K und H hängt
nicht davon ab, ob man die modernen naturalistischen Gehaltstheorien für
überzeugend oder relevant hält.

6. Stimmungen und körperliche Gefühle

Um meinen Vermittlungsversuch noch ein Stück voranzutreiben, möchte ich
schließlich einige weiteren mentalen Phänomene in Betracht ziehen, die
Anlass zum Streit zwischen Intentionalisten und Antiintentionalisten gegeben
haben. Wenden wir uns zuerst den *Stimmungen* zu. Es wird häufig behauptet,
Stimmungen wie Depression oder Angst seien *gegenstandslos* und somit ein
klares Beispiel für nichtintentionale mentale Zustände. Nicht selten beruft man
sich dabei auf Kierkegaards oder Heideggers Analysen der Angst. Aber auch
analytische Philosophen haben in jüngerer Zeit den nichtintentionalen
Charakter der Stimmungen hervorgehoben.[67]

Bei näherem Hinsehen zeigt es sich aber erneut, dass der Konflikt
weitgehend terminologisch ist. Die Intentionalisten geben mehr oder weniger
offen zu, dass Stimmungen keinen Gegenstand im engeren – und üblichen –
Sinne haben. Das – und nicht mehr – ist es aber auch, was die Antiintentionalisten mit ihrer Rede von der Gegenstandslosigkeit gemeint haben. Sie haben
selbstverständlich nicht leugnen wollen, dass Stimmungen einen bestimmten
Charakter besitzen, dass sie dem Subjekt etwas bedeuten oder dass sie seine
intentionalen Erlebnisse beeinflussen. Man darf nicht vergessen, dass es
gerade die angeblichen Antiintentionalisten waren, die auf die besondere
Bedeutung von Stimmungen zuerst aufmerksam machten und somit gegen

eine Auffassung der Kognition rebellierten, der zufolge sie eine emotionslose Beziehung zu "nackten" Tatsachen sei und Wissen und Emotionen somit nichts miteinander zu tun hätten. Die Existenzphilosophen haben die Stimmungen in den Mittelpunkt gerückt, weil sie meinten, dass sie für die Selbsterkenntnis – und indirekt auch für die Metaphysik im allgemeinen – relevant sind. Sie messen ihnen also offensichtlich einen Erkenntniswert zu.

Nicht von ungefähr werden Stimmungen häufig mit *Farben* verglichen:[68] Sie verleihen den wahrgenommen Gegenständen eine besondere, zusätzliche Qualität und lässt die ganze Situation gleichsam in einem anderen Licht erscheinen, ohne jedoch an den objektiven Eigenschaften des Repräsentierten etwas zu ändern. So gesehen sind sie – ebenso wie Farbempfindungen und Schmerzen – durchaus repräsentationsrelevant (d.h. sie haben einen intentionalen Wert), aber nicht intentional im prägnanten Sinne, da sie das Subjekt nicht mit einem eigenen, distinkten Gegenstand konfrontieren.

Nehmen wir Heidegger als Beispiel. Er behauptet zwar, das "Wovor der Angst" sei völlig unbestimmt,[69] die Angst "enthülle" das Nichts und das Nichts werde "nicht als Gegenstand gegeben.[70] All das klingt natürlich sehr antiintentionalistisch. Aber Heidegger betont gleichzeitig, dass die Angst immerhin ein distinktes Phänomen und für den Weltbezug im Allgemeinen bedeutsam ist:

> Die völlige Unbedeutsamkeit, die sich im Nichts und Nirgends bekundet, bedeutet nicht Weltabwesenheit, sondern besagt, dass das innerweltlich Seiende an ihm selbst so völlig belanglos ist, dass auf dem Grunde dieser *Unbedeutsamkeit* des Innerweltlichen die Welt in ihrer Weltlichkeit sich einzig noch aufdrängt ... Allein dieses Nichts von Zuhandenem ... ist kein totales Nichts. Das Nichts von Zuhandenheit gründet im ursprünglichsten "Etwas", in der *Welt.*[71]

Es wäre somit ein Missverständnis zu glauben, in Stimmungen wie Angst komme nach Ansicht der Existenzphilosophen überhaupt *nichts zum Vorschein.*

Selbstverständlich unterscheiden die existenzphilosophischen Analysen sich in mehreren Hinsichten von denen der heutigen Intentionalisten. Dennoch gibt es beachtliche Parallelen. Michael Tye sagt z.B.:

> Mood experiences, I maintain, like emotions, are sensory representations. What exactly they represent is not easy to pin down, but the general picture I have is as follows: ... When moods descend on us, we are responding in a sensory way to a *departure* from the pertinent range of physical states. We are sensing physical changes in our 'body landscapes" ...[72]

> With moods ... the relevant qualities are usually not experienced as located ... If one feels elated, one experiences a change in oneself *overall*. The qualities of which one is directly aware in attending to how one feels on such an occasion are experienced as qualities of *oneself*. One is aware of a general sense of buoyancy, of quickened reactions, of somehow being more alive.[73]

Tye gibt also zu, dass Stimmungen und Emotionen in einer deutlich anderen Weise als Wahrnehmungen repräsentieren; dass es häufig schwierig ist zu sagen, *was* genau sie repräsentieren; und dass ihr Objekt in jedem Fall ein sehr unbestimmtes bleibt, wie etwa der "Gesamtzustand" unseres Körpers. Dies ist gar nicht so weit von Heideggers Auffassung entfernt, Stimmungen seien verschiedene Modi der "Befindlichkeit" des Menschen und zeigten, in welcher Verfassung er sei. Freilich fällt auf, dass bei Heidegger und seinen Gleichgesinnten nicht wie bei Tye von einem *körperlichen* Gesamtzustand die Rede ist. Aber wie groß – und wie bedeutsam – ist dieser Unterschied eigentlich? Ein Anhänger der traditionellen heideggerschen Auffassung könnte wohl ohne Schwierigkeiten zugeben, dass Stimmungen auch einen körperlichen Aspekt haben – dass der Mensch qua körperliches Wesen seine allgemeine Situation und Verfassung sowohl *mittels* seines Körpers als auch diesen *betreffend* erlebt. Dass Emotionen und Wahrnehmungen von Veränderungen im eigenen Körper eng miteinander verbunden sind, ist ohnehin eine weit verbreitete Ansicht (in der Psychologie ist sie als die *James-Lange-These* bekannt), die nicht unbedingt intentionalistisch gedeutet werden muss.

Auf jeden Fall wäre es nicht plausibel zu behaupten, dass die Stimmungen in einem prägnanteren Sinne den körperlichen Zustand des Subjekts *repräsentierten*. Tye scheint dies *de facto* selbst zuzugeben, wenn er den "Gegenstand" einer gehobenen Stimmung als ein "allgemeines Gefühl, irgendwie mehr lebendig zu sein" beschreibt. Dies klingt nicht gerade wie die Beschreibung eines physiologischen Sachverhaltes. Es klingt vielmehr wie ein stillschweigendes Akzept der – angeblich antiintentionalistischen – Auffassung der Existenzphilosophen: Der "Gegenstand" der Stimmungen ist nicht etwas, das als rein körperlich erlebt wird, auch wenn das Erlebnis zweifelsohne Momente körperlicher Empfindung enthält.

Nachdem wir zu dieser Auffassung gelangt sind, lohnt es sich, nochmals einen Blick auf verwandte mentale Phänomene wie Lust und Schmerz zu werfen. Denn könnte es nicht sein, dass ihre scheinbar nichtintentionalen Varianten – wie z.B. Orgasmus – ebenfalls einen Gesamtzustand des Subjektes repräsentierten? Wäre es nicht richtig zu sagen, dass ein Orgasmus die sonstigen Wahrnehmungen des Subjektes – einschließlich die von Tye hervorgehobenen Empfindung vom Zustand der Genitalien – gleichsam "färben" oder "durchdringen"?[74] Wenn eine solche (zugegebenermaßen metaphorische)[75] Beschreibung akzeptabel wäre, dann könnte man als nächstes den Fall der Schmerzen neu überdenken. Auch hier wäre es vielleicht ratsam, die Suche nach einem distinkten, "lokalen" physiologischen Korrelat aufzugeben, aber daran festzuhalten, dass Schmerz eine im weiteren Sinne körperliche Empfindung ist, da er auf jeden Fall das Subjekt mit seiner eigenen negativen Verfassung bekannt macht. Tim Crane hat ähnlich argumentiert. Er lehnt Tyes These, die Gegenstände von Schmerzen seien *Körperverletzungen*, als zu restriktiv ab.[76] Seiner Meinung nach ist ihr Bezug auf den Körper von einer loseren und vageren Art:

> The point is not that a sensation must be felt to occupy a non-vague relatively circumscribed location, but that it is felt to be somewhere within one's body.[77]

Es sind wohlgemerkt nicht nur die Intentionalisten, die Zugeständnisse machen müssen. Mein Vorschlag läuft auf einen genuinen Kompromiss hinaus. Das wird am Beispiel der sogenannten "Nachbilder" (*afterimages*) deutlich. Die Antiintentionalisten bemerken zwar treffend, dass sie nicht als Objekte im engeren Sinne – als Gegenstände "in der Welt" – erlebt werden.[78] Aber dies wiederspricht nur einem sehr restriktiven E-Intentionalismus. Und die Intentionalisten behaupten zurecht, dass sie nichtsdestotrotz als Objekte erlebt werden – als etwas, das eine oder mehrere Eigenschaften besitzt. Tye zufolge repräsentieren Nachbilder, "dass etwas anwesend ist mit einer gewissen zweidimensionalen Form und einer Farbe".[79] Das ist ein gutes Beispiel dafür, dass selbst sehr primitive und nebensächliche mentale Phänomene im weiten Sinne intentional sein können, aber dass ihnen nicht deswegen einen äußeren Gegenstand oder eine sonstige externe Beziehung zugeschrieben werden muss.[80]

7. Konklusion

Mein Kompromissvorschlag lautet also wie folgt: Die Kernthese des Intentionalismus – dass es keinen Unterschied im phänomenalen Charakter eines mentalen Zustandes geben kann ohne einen entsprechenden Unterschied in seinem intentionalen Gehalt – ist durchaus korrekt. Der weitergehenden Hauptthese, alle mentale Zustände seien intentional, sollte man dagegen nicht vorbehaltlos zustimmen. Es gibt vermutlich mentale Zustände, die nicht intentional im vollen, prägnanten Sinne des Wortes sind. Sie sind aber wenigstens protointentional, d.h. sie liefern einen Beitrag zum intentionalen Gehalt. Ob wir uns für H1 oder H2 entscheiden sollen, hängt also davon ab, ob wir den Begriff der Intentionalität in einem weiten oder engeren Sinn verwenden möchten. Angesichts des heutigen Diskussionsklimas, in dem "Intentionalität" häufig mit dem E-Intentionalismus assoziiert wird, ziehe ich es vor, den Begriff für die prägnanten Fälle von Intentionalität zu reservieren und somit diejenigen Zustände, die keinen eigenen, wohldefinierten Gegenstand haben, als nichtintentional zu bezeichnen.

Vieles scheint für K3 zu sprechen. Es wäre aber auch möglich, die zusätzlichen strukturellen Elemente (und die sensorische Modalität), auf denen die Intentionalität vermutlich superveniert, zum phänomenalen Charakter im weitem Sinne zu rechnen. Mithilfe eines solchen – eher phänomenologischen als phänomenalistischen – Begriffs des Phänomenalen könnte K2 auch akzeptiert werden. Und wenn man sowohl den Phänomenbegriff als auch den Intentionalitätsbegriff sehr weit fassen würde, dann ließe sich K1 sogar aufrechterhalten, da die beiden Faktoren als identisch betrachtet werden könnten und die Supervenienzrelation somit symmetrisch wäre.

Was den E-Intentionalismus betrifft, so bleibt mein Vorschlag ihm gegenüber im Prinzip neutral, obwohl man zweifeln haben kann, wie gut er mit einem eher phänomenologisch fundierten Intentionalismus harmoniert. Ob die Einbeziehung externalistischer Gehaltstheorien zu einer Neubestimmung des Phänomenalen führt, die mit seiner traditionellen Charakterisierung nicht unbedingt kompatibel ist, bleibt dahingestellt.

Wenn ich recht habe, stimmt es also nicht, dass der Gegensatz zwischen Intentionalisten und Antiintentionalisten "die größte Kluft in der Philosophie des Geistes" ist, wie Ned Block meint.[81] Er ist gar keine Kluft, sondern es handelt sich hauptsächlich um Nuancenunterschiede, verschiedene terminologische Präferenzen und nicht zuletzt um verschiedene metaphysische Hintergedanken. Über die konkrete Beschreibung der mentalen Zustände ist man sich weitgehend einig. Dies bedeutet selbstverständlich nicht, dass es in der heutigen Philosophie des Geistes keine echte Streitfragen oder tiefe Gegensätze gäbe. Nur handelt es sich um andere, benachbarte, aber prinzipiell unabhängige Kontroversen. Eine solche ist der Streit zwischen Externalisten und Internalisten. Sicherlich spielt das alte Leib-Seele-Problem auch noch eine Rolle. Obwohl die meisten es für mehr oder weniger überwunden halten und es kaum noch erklärte Dualisten gibt, hängt vieles weiterhin davon ab, wie weit man bereit ist, den dualistischen Intuitionen zu folgen. Die tiefste und bedeutsamste Kluft scheint mir jedoch die zwischen einer "intrinsikalistischen" und einer "extrinsikalistischen" Betrachtungsweise zu sein.[82] Auf der einen Seite gibt es Philosophen, die wie Block, Searle und die verbliebenen Dualisten und Kryptodualisten darauf beharren, dass der phänomenale Charakter eines mentalen Zustands nicht durch seine "horizontalen" Beziehungen (sei es funktionale, kausale oder teleologische) konstituiert wird. Auf der anderen Seite gibt es die Funktionalisten und E-Intentionalisten, die den phänomenalen Charakter für eine echte relationale – und somit extrinsische – Eigenschaft halten. Die erste Fraktion streitet sich intern darüber, inwiefern die phänomenalen Zustände über ihre "vertikalen" Beziehungen zu physikalischen Tatsachen doch reduzierbar sind. Innerhalb der zweiten scheiden sich die Meinungen hinsichtlich der Frage, welche Art von Relationen wahrhaft konstitutiv sind. Wenn es nur um die Intentionalität der phänomenalen Zuständen geht, stimmen die Meinungen aller Parteien weitgehend überein.

Anmerkungen

1. Vor allem Tye (1995) versteht den Intentionalismus in dieser Weise. Auch Dretske (1995a) und mit Vorbehalt Harman (1990) und Lycan (1996) sind der Ansicht, Bewusstsein lasse sich durch seine repräsentierende Funktion vollständig erklären. Byrne (2001) beschränkt sich auf die These, alles Bewusstsein sei ntentional, und nimmt keine Stellung zur Frage der Reduzierbarkeit. Crane (2001) lehnt sogar die Möglichkeit einer Reduktion von Bewusstsein auf rein physikalische Eigenschaften ausdrücklich ab; seine Version des Intentionalismus ist deutlich anti-physikalistisch. Jacquette (1994) verteidigt eine ähnliche Kombination von Eigenschaftsdualismus und Internalismus.
2. Vgl. Tye 2000, p. 45; Byrne 2001, p. 204
3. Vgl. etwa Peacocke 1983 und Block 1993
4. Ned Block betont somit, dass die eigentliche Streitfrage sei, ob Erlebnisse *weitere* Elemente als ihren intentionalen Gehalt hätten (1995, pp. 26f.). Er stimmt mit dem Intentionalismus darin überein, dass Empfindungen häufig – vielleicht sogar immer – intentional seien und dass sie ihren intentionalen Gehalt Kraft ihrer phänomenalen Charakter hätten (1995, p. 20).
5. Ein Beispiel dafür sind Tyes Überlegungen zur "Transparenz" des phänomenalen Bewusstseins (2000, pp. 45ff.)
6. *Logische Untersuchungen* II/1, §§14-15
7. Vgl. etwa McGinn 1982, p. 8; Rosenthal 1994, p. 349
8. LU II/1, V, §14 (Husserliana XIX/1, p. 397)

9. LU II/1, V, §14 (Husserliana XIX/1, p. 399)
10. LU II/1, V, §15b (Husserliana XIX/1, p. 406)
11. LU II/1, V, §15b (Husserliana XIX/1, p. 406)
12. Tye 1995, p. 113; Crane 2001, p. 79ff.
13. LU II/1, V, §14 (Husserliana XIX/1, pp. 395ff.)
14. LU II/2, VI, §9 (Husserliana XIX/2, pp. 570ff.)
15. LU II/1, V, §14 (Husserliana XIX/1, p. 395)
16. LU II/1, V, §14 (Husserliana XIX/1, pp. 396f.)
17. Vgl. dazu Crane 2001, pp. 18ff; 28ff.
18. LU II/1, I, §23, (Husserliana XIX/1, p. 80)
19. Frege: 'Der Gedanke', 1986, p. 51
20. Vgl. Dummett 1988, p. 76f.
21. Vgl. 'Simple Seeing', Dretske 2000, pp. 97-112
22. Husserls *Erfahrung und Urteil* enthält die vielleicht ausführlichste Argumentation für die Existenz vorpropositionaler (und vorbegrifflicher) Erfahrung in der klassischen ("voranalytischen") Philosophie des Geistes. Dieselbe Auffassung ist in der gegenwärtigen Debatte u.a. von Holenstein 1980, Fales 1996, Klausen 1997 und Schantz 2001 verteidigt worden.
23. Marcus Willaschek hat gegen Dretskes Theorie der nichtbegrifflichen Wahrnehmung eingewendet, dass sie eher von der *Zuschreibung* von Wahrnehmungen handele als von Wahrnehmungen an sich. Wenn wir von einem nichtbegrifflichen Sehen sprächen, identifizierten wir den Gegenstand gleichsam von außen, d.h. wir beschreiben ihn mithilfe unserer *eigenen* Begriffen. In dieser Weise kann man zwar sagen, dass ein Ureinwohner Neuguineas einen Kühlschrank sieht, obwohl er nicht über den Begriff Kühlschrank verfügt. Aber dabei erfasst man den eigentlichen (subjektiven) Gehalt seiner Wahrnehmung gar nicht (Willaschek 2001, pp. 270f.).
Ein strukturell ähnliches Argument ist von Tim Crane gegen den semantischen Externalismus vorgebracht worden: Der Externalismus mag als eine Theorie unserer *Zuschreibungspraxis* richtig sein, nicht aber als eine Theorie über die Inhalte unserer Gedanken *per se*, d.h. über ihre intrinsischen Eigenschaften (Crane 2001, pp. 114ff.). Obwohl ich den letzteren Einwand für zutreffend halte, finde ich, dass Willaschecks Argument zu kurz greift. Denn es gibt m.E. einen klaren Sinn, indem der Ureinwohner tatsächlich einen Kühlschrank sieht: er hat ein eigentümliches visuelles Erlebnis, indem ihm etwas in der für einen Kühlschrank typischen Weise (d.h. mit den für einen Kühlschrank typischen Eigenschaften) erscheint. Er hat nicht nur vereinzelte Empfindungen, die auf eine Konzeptualisierung warten, sondern nimmt von Anfang an einen bestimmten Gegenstand wahr; er erlebt sozusagen etwas "Kühlschrankiges", oder, anders gesagt, er lernt den *Stereotyp* eines Kühlschrankes kennen, der als Basis für die Konzeptualisierung dient. Vgl. dazu Fales 1996, p. 105; Schantz 2001, p. 257
24. Ein markantes Beispiel für diese Zwischenposition ist die Auffassung von H. H. Price: "... there are forms of consciousness in which recognition of characteristics occurs but recognition of individuals does not. On the other hand, without the capacity of recognizing some characteristics at least, however dimly, mental life would not exist at all … [or at] any rate … it would be absolutely useless to its possessor" (1953, p. 41).
25. Vgl. dazu Mulligan 1995, pp. 183f.
26. Fallstudien aus der empirischen Psychopathologie deuten jedoch darauf hin, dass diese Behauptung falsch ist. Vgl. Sacks 1985, pp. 42ff.
27. Eine solche Auffassung von Selbstbewusstsein ist u.a. von Dieter Henrich (1970), Manfred Frank (1986) und Erich Klawonn (1987) vertreten worden.
28. Block 1995, p. 37

29. Henrich (1986) betont, dass sogar das rudimentärste, vorreflexive Selbstbewusstsein eine solche Komplexität besitzt. Ähnliche Überlegungen finden sich beim späten Husserl, z.B. in seinen C-Manuskripten.
30. Searle (1983, pp. 2f.) betont, dass das "of" im Ausdruck "experience of anxiety" eine andere, nichtintentionale Bedeutung als das "of" im Ausdruck "fear of snakes". Denn im ersten Fall sind das Erlebnis und sein Objekt gewissermaßen identisch (oder genauer gesagt: Das Objekt ist ein Moment des Erlebnisses). Man könnte aber auch sagen – mit Crane (2001, pp. 78f.) – dass bereits das erste "of" Intentionalität ausdrückt, weil es doch eine Struktur repräsentiert, die ein Subjekt, ein besonderer Modus des Erlebens und einen besonderen Gehalt (d.h. eine besondere Gegebenheitsweise) einschließt (2001, pp. 28ff.). So gesehen ist die Frage rein terminologisch. Sie ist aber trotzdem von Bedeutung, weil viele Intentionalisten im Laufe ihrer Untersuchen den weiten, harmlosen Begriff der Intentionalität durch einen engeren mehr oder weniger stillschweigend ersetzen.
31. Brentano 1924, p. 124
32. Brentano 192, p. 114
33. Brentano 1924, p. 124
34. Vgl. dazu Bell 1990, p. 8. Diese Charakterisierung trifft allerdings nur auf Brentanos frühe Position (in der *Psychologie vom empirischen Standpunkt*) zu.
35. Vgl. etwa Tye 1995, p. 96
36. Tye 1995, p. 101.
37. Dretske 1995a, p. 7
38. Vgl. Tye 1995a, pp. 5ff.; 103f.; 142f.
39. Tye 1995, p. 144 (Box 5.4)
40. Tye 2000, p. 172
41. Brentano 1924, p. 125
42. Brentano 1924, p. 128
43. Brentano 1924, p. 127
44. Searle 1983, p. 2
45. Brentano 1924, pp. 125ff.
46. Natürlich kann man auch Reduktionist und Intentionalist sein, ohne eine externalistische Gehaltstheorie zu vertreten. Aber in diesem Fall bleibt die Verbindung zwischen Intentionalismus und Reduktionismus rein äußerlich.
47. Crane (2001, p. 17) vertritt eine ähnliche Auffassung.
48. Ein gutes Beispiel dafür ist Ruth Millikan (1984, p. 12)
49. Eine Ausnahme bilden die mehr oder weniger neo-Fregeanischen Versionen des Externalismus, z.B. die Theorien von Evans, Peacocke und McDowell. Da sie aber keine naturalistische Reduktion des intentionalen Gehaltes ermöglichen, sind sie aber in diesem Zusammenhang irrelevant.
50. Vgl. Dretske 1995b
51. Vgl. etwa Burge 1997
52. Dretske 1995a, p. 8
53. Vgl. etwa Putnam 1975, p. 226 und insbesondere Burge 1979
54. Vgl. dazu Goldman 1993
55. Vgl. Millikan: 'Biosemantics', 1993, p. 84
56. Vgl. etwa Dretske 1981, pp. 171ff.
57. Tye 1995, p. 101
58. Vgl. Fodor 1987, p. 105; Millikan: 'Compare and Contrast Dretske, Fodor, and Millikan on Teleosemantics', 1993, p. 124

59. Vlg. Crane 2001, p. 144
60. Vgl. 'Compare and Contrast Dretske, Fodor, and Millikan on Teleosemantics', 1993, p. 127
61. Vgl. etwa Fodor 1990
62. Tye 1995, pp. 153ff.; 2000, pp. 119ff.
63. Tye greift in diesem Fall doch auf die evolutionäre Erklärung zurück (1995, p. 153). Aber eine "gemischte" Theorie, der zufolge der Gehalt manchmal von der Evolutionsgeschichte, manchmal aber (wenn die Evolutionsgeschichte fehlt) von ahistorischen Dispositionen abhängt, ist allzu offensichtlich *ad hoc* und macht es zweifelhaft, ob der Gehalt überhaupt eine reale Größe ist.
64. Tye 1995, p. 101
65. Vgl. Tye 2000, p. 122
66. Tye 1995, pp. 134f.
67. Vgl. etwa Searle 1992, p. 140. Auch Dretske gibt interessanterweise zu, dass Stimmungen nicht unmittelbar intentional sind (1995, p. 103)
68. Vgl. z.B. Searle 1992, p. 140. John Haugeland vergleicht sie mit Dämpfen (*vapors*) (1985, p. 235)
69. Heidegger 1986, p. 186
70. Heidegger 1967, p. 112
71. Heidegger 1986, p. 187
72. Tye 1995, p. 129
73. Tye 2000, p. 51
74. Haugeland (1985, p. 235) verwendet eine ähnliche Metapher (*seep into*) bei seiner Beschreibung von Stimmungen
75. Es ist zu beachten, dass *alle* Diskussionsteilnehmer Stimmungen und ähnliche Phänomene metaphorisch oder indirekt beschreiben. Dies gilt nicht weniger für Tye als für die Existenzphilosophen.
76. Crane 2001, p. 85
77. Crane 2001, p. 79
78. Vgl. z.B. Boghossian and Velleman 1989
79. Tye 1995, p. 108
80. Tye behauptet interessanterweise auch, dass Nachbilder immer illusorisch sind, da ihre Gegenstände gar nicht existieren (1995, p. 109). Offenkundig lockert sich dadurch die Verbindung zwischen der Intentionalität phänomenaler Zustände mit der kausalen Kovariation, die Tye sonst für konstitutiv hält.
81. Block 1995, p. 19
82. Goldman (1993) macht eine ähnliche Unterscheidung.

Literatur

Bell, David: 1990, *Husserl*, Routledge, London

Block, Ned: 1993, 'Review of D. Dennett, *Consciousness Explained*', *Journal of Philosophy* 90, 181-193

Block, Ned: 1995, 'Mental Paint and Mental Latex, in Villanueva 1995, 19-49

Block, Ned, Flanagan, Owen & Güzeldere, Güven (Hrsg.): 1997. *The Nature of Consciousness*, MIT Press, Cambridge, Mass.

Block, Ned: 1998, 'Is Experiencing Just Representing?', *Philosophy and Phenomenological Research* 58, 663-70

Boghossian, Paul & Velleman, J. David: 1989, 'Colour as a Secondary Quality', *Mind* 98, 81-103

Brentano, Franz: 1924, *Psychologie vom empirischen Standpunkt. Erster Band*, Felix Meiner, Hamburg

Burge, Tyler: 1979, 'Individualism and the Mental', *Midwest Studies in Philosophy* 5, 73-122

Burge, Tyler: 1997, 'Two Kinds of Consciousness', in Block et al. 1997, 427-33

Byrne, Alex: 2001, 'Intentionalism Defended', *Philosophical Review* 110, 199-240 Crane, Tim: 2001, *Elements of Mind*, Oxford University Press, Oxford

Dretske, Fred: 1981, *Knowledge and the Flow of Information*, MIT Press, Cambridge, Mass.

Dretske, Fred: 1995a, *Naturalizing the Mind*, MIT Press, Cambridge, Mass.

Dretske, Fred: 1995b, 'Phenomenal Externalism or If Meanings Ain't in the Head, Where Are Qualia?', in Villanueva 1995, 143-158

Dretske, Fred: 2000, *Perception, Knowledge and Belief. Selected Essays*, Cambridge University Press, Cambridge

Dummett, Michael: 1988, *Ursprünge der analytischen Philosophie*, Suhrkamp, Frankfurt a. M.

Fales, Evan: 1996, *A Defence of the Given*, Rowman & Littlefield, Lanham

Fodor, Jerry: 1987, *Psychosemantics*, MIT Press, Cambridge, Mass.

Fodor, Jerry: 1990, 'A Theory of Content, I: The Problem', in *A Theory of Content and Other Essays*, MIT Press, Cambridge, Mass., 51-87

Frank, Manfred: 1986, *Die Unhintergehbarkeit von Individualität*, Suhrkamp, Frankfurt a. M.

Frege, Gottlob: 1986, *Logische Untersuchungen* (hrsg. von G. Patzig), Vandenhoeck & Ruprecht, Göttingen

Goldman, Alvin I. 1993. 'Consciousness, Folk Psychology and Cognitive Science', *Consciousness and Cognition* 2: 364-382

Grundmann, Thomas (Hrsg.): 2001, *Erkenntnistheorie. Positionen zwischen Tradition und Gegenwart*, Mentis Verlag, Paderborn

Guttenplan, Samuel (Hrsg): 1994, *A Companion to the Philosophy of Mind*, Blackwell, Oxford

Harman, Gilbert: 1990, 'The Intrinsic Quality of Experience', *Philosophical Perspectives* Vol. 4, ed. J. Tomberlin, Northridge, CA, 31-52

Haugeland, John: 1985, *Artificial Intelligence: The Very Idea*, MIT Press, Cambridge, Mass.

Heidegger, Martin: 1967, 'Was ist Metaphysik?', in *Wegmarken*, Vittorio Klostermann, Frankfurt a. M., 103-121

Heidegger, Martin: 1986, *Sein und Zeit*, Max Niemeyer, Tübingen

Henrich, Dieter: 1970, 'Selbstbewusstsein. Kritische Einleitung in eine Theorie', in Bubner et al. (Hrsg): *Hermeneutik und Dialektik* I-II, J.C.B. Mohr, Tübingen

Henrich, Dieter: 1985, 'Selbstbewusstsein. Ein Problemfeld mit offener Grenzen', *Berichte aus der Forschung* 68 (München).

Holenstein, Elmar: 1980, *Von der Hintergehbarkeit der Sprache*, Suhrkamp, Frankfurt a. M.

Husserl, Edmund: 1984, *Logische Untersuchungen* II/1 & II/2 (*Husserliana* XIX/1 & XIX/2), Martinus Nijhoff, Den Haag

Husserl, Edmund: 1985, *Erfahrung und Urteil* (hrsg. von L. Landgrebe), Felix Meiner, Hamburg

Jacquette, Dale: 1994, *Philosophy of Mind*, Englewood Cliffs, NJ.

Klausen, Søren Harnow: 1997, *Verfahren oder Gegebenheit?*, Attempto, Tübingen

Klawonn, Erich: 1987, 'The I: On the Ontology of First Person Identity', *Danish Yearbook of Philosophy* 24

Lycan, William: 1996, *Consciousness and Experience*, MIT Press, Cambridge, Mass.

Millikan, Ruth Garrett: 1984, *Language, Thought and Other Biological Categories*, Cambridge, Mass.

Millikan, Ruth Garrett: 1993, *White Queen Psychology and Other Essays for Alice*, MIT Press, Cambridge, Mass.

Mulligan, Kevin: 1995, 'Perception', in Smith, B. & Smith, David W. (Hrsg.): *The Cambridge Companion to Husserl*, Cambridge University Press, Cambridge, 168-238

Peacocke, Christopher: 1983, *Sense and Content*, Oxford University Press, Oxford

Price, H. H.: 1953, *Thinking and Experience*, Hutchinson, London

Putnam, Hilary: 1975, 'The Meaning of "Meaning"', *Mind, Language and Reality*, Cambridge University Press, Cambridge, 215-271

Rosental, David M.: 1994, 'Identity Theories', in Guttenplan 1994, 348-355

Sacks, Oliver: 1985, *The Man Who Mistook His Wife for a Hat*, Duckworth, London

Schantz, Richard: 2001, 'Der Inhalt der Erfahrung', in Grundmann 2001, 249-263

Searle, John R.: 1983, *Intentionality*, Cambridge University Press, Cambridge

Searle, John R.: 1992, *The Rediscovery of the Mind*, MIT Press, Cambridge, Mass.

Tye, Michael: 1995, *Ten Problems of Consciousness*, MIT Press, Cambridge, Mass.

Tye, Michael: 2000, *Consciousness, Colour and Content*. MIT Press, Cambridge, Mass.

Villanueva, Enrique (Hrsg.): 1995, *Philosophical Issues* 7, Northridge, CA

Willaschek, Marcus; 2001, 'Phänomenale Begriffsverwendung und die Rechtfertigungsfunktion der Wahrnehmung', in Grundmann 2001, 264-282

Danish Yearbook of Philosophy, Vol. 40 (2005), 109-144

THE TURING TEST: AN EXAMINATION OF ITS NATURE AND ITS MENTALISTIC ONTOLOGY

CHRISTIAN BEENFELDT

University of Copenhagen

I. Exordium

We live in a culture that, within a mere half-century has become saturated by a panoply of computer technology – from the ubiquity of the personal computer and the globally reticulated Internet, to the sublunary existence of data satellites and the embedded presence of information technology in entertainment devices, cars, airplanes, medical instruments and soon, perhaps, also in our very bodies. Coetaneous with this development, *the question of machine intelligence* has arisen in the study of mind – a question that was famously posed by the British mathematician Alan Turing while the early behemothian digital computers were still in their very infancy.

> "I propose to consider the question, 'Can machines think?'"

Thus begins Turing's paper, *Computing Machinery and Intelligence*, which appeared in *Mind* in 1950 and introduced what has subsequently become known as the *Turing Test*. The paper is widely recognized to have exercised a vast influence both upon the philosophy of mind and upon the then fledgling fields of cognitive science and artificial intelligence. Assessments of its influence include the following:

Moor:

> Fifty years ago Alan Turing published his famous article "Computing Machinery and Intelligence" in the journal *Mind*. This article is arguably the most influential and widely read article in the philosophy of artificial intelligence... His vision of the possibility of machine intelligence has been highly inspiring and extremely controversial.[1]

French:

> Turing's article has unquestionably generated more commentary and controversy than any other article in the field of artificial intelligence with few papers in any field creating such an enduring reaction.[2]
>
> It is arguably one of the most widely discussed scientific papers ever written.[3]

Preston:

> 'Computing Machinery and Intelligence' is surely the most famous, most widely read and reprinted, and the most influential article ever to have been published in a philosophy journal.[4]

While Turing seemed have intended his test to settle the question of machine thinking in a fairly straightforward manner – offering a "philosophical conversation-stopper", as Daniel Dennett puts it – the antipodean state of affairs has nevertheless ensued. Far from proroguing the discussion, the test sparked a highly controversial and prolific debate that has lasted more than half a century so far, and has involved a number of different fields – from philosophy, artificial intelligence and cognitive science to psychology and communication studies.

In 2000, as the test passed the half-century mark since its introduction, its continuing relevance to the contemporary debate was underscored by the fact that an entire issue of the journal *Mind and Machines* was dedicated to it. Two years later, Oxford University Press published *Views Into the Chinese Room*, a collection of articles by such renowned philosophers and cognitive scientists as Ned Block, Stevan Harnad, Terry Winograd, Jack Copeland, Roger Penrose and John Haugeland, pertaining to John Searle's Chinese Room Argument – a Gedankenexperiment which derives its fame from challenging the assumption of Turing's (and, subsequently, also of many other thinkers in artificial intelligence and cognitive science) that an appropriately programmed computer, by virtue of the program it is instantiating, really would have a mind of its own.

Those are merely two recent highpoints drawn from the substantial fabric of cross-disciplinary discussion involving the Turing Test. To point out a few intertwined threads in this plentiful garment, one could mention the following: the debate about the operational or inductive nature of the test;[5] the discussion of the level of intelligence ascribed by the test (discussed below); the question of the gender identity of the being imitated;[6] the challenge of the Chinese

Room Argument;[7] the relationship of the test and the psychological issues of paranoia,[8] naïve psychology[9] and subcognition;[10] and, finally, the issues of underdetermination, functional indistinguishability and robotic upgrades, as applied to the test.[11]

The discussion has not, furthermore, been purely theoretical. Since 1991 the Turing Test has been implemented in practice at the annual Loebner Prize Contest – a contest begun by Hugh Loebner and the Cambridge Center for Behavioral Studies in 1991, originally offering $100,000 and a solid gold medal to the first successful candidate.

As rule nr. 1 of the contest states:

> The objective of the Loebner Prize Competition in Artificial Intelligence is to identify the computer system that can best succeed in passing a modern variant of the Turing Test.[12]

Former administers of the test at this event have included a string of renowned figures, such as: I. Bernard Cohen, Daniel Dennett, Robert Epstein, Harry Lewis, Allen Newell, Willard Van Orman Quine and Joseph Weizenbaum.[13]

Regarding the overall influence of the test on artificial intelligence, cognitive science and related fields, Dale Jacquette describes it as follows:

> The idea that the mind is a machine, the research program to reduce or explain mind in terms of purely mechanical operations, and the design of artificial intelligence that models or duplicates human intelligence, have for many years takes their direction and inspiration from the Turing Test. [14]

To afford a comprehensive understanding of this influential test, the following three questions must reasonably be afforded an answer:

1. What *exactly is* the Turing Test?
2. What *assumptions* does the Turing Test rest on?
3. What are the *objections* to the Turing Test?

The goal of this paper is to contribute to the answering of the first two questions (in sections I-IV and V-IX, respectively), thereby aiming to further clarify the influential and wide-reaching debate encompassing the many objections and replies pertaining to the test.

Let us proceed with a very short recapitulation of the test.

II. The Imitation Game

Immediately following the breviloquent introductory sentence of *Computing Machinery and Intelligence*, Turing acknowledges that a consideration of machine thinking should begin with a definition of the terms "machine" and "think". Yet, he asserts, a definition according to normal usage of those terms would be absurd, since it would imply that the answer is to be found in a statistical survey such as the Gallup poll. Sidestepping this approach altogether, he suggests a replacement of the ambiguous question "Can machines think?" by a closely related one, expressed in relatively unambiguous words. This replacement requires a description of the imitation game.

> It is played with three people, a man (A), a woman (B), and an interrogator (C) who may be of either sex. The interrogator stays in a room apart from the other two. The object of the game for the interrogator is to determine which of the other two is the man and which is the woman. He knows them by labels X and Y, and at the end of the game he says either 'X is A and Y is B' or 'X is B and Y is A'.[15]

The question "can machines think?" will then be replaced by the question:

> What will happen when a machine takes the part of A in this game? Will the interrogator decide wrongly as often when the game is played like this as he does when the game is played between a man and a woman?[16]

This new question thus involves the following elements:

1. A text-only communication link between (A) and (B) on one side of a physical barrier, and (C) on the other.
2. The attempt by both (A) and (B) to convince (C) that he/she/it is a person, not a machine.[17]
3. The challenge to (C) to determine which is the person and which is the machine.

This approach to the question of machine thinking, then, avoids construing the problem as an issue of mere linguistic usage, to be resolved by appeal to either vox populi or to a linguistic analysis of the meaning of the terms involved. Rather, in formulating an experiment of sorts, as the means of ascertaining machine thinking, Turing intends to direct our attention to the empirical matter at hand and away from the enmeshment of language and usage. In a related manner, Turing also breaks with the tradition of formulating phenomenological descriptions of the mental landscape as they introspectively appear to the subject – as manifested historically in the philosophy of mind, for example, by early 20th century introspectionism. In more recent terminology, then, we may say that the Turing Test represents an attempt to formulate a test of (mechanized) other minds while circumventing what Chalmers famously calls the "hard" problem of consciousness – the problem of explaining the subjective aspect of every experience, i.e. of explaining phenomenal consciousness, qualia or "what it is like to be", in Nagel's famous words. In compliance with the mid-20th century influence of methodological behaviorism, the Turing Test affords the ascription of a highly complex mental phenomenon – such as "intelligence" or the ability to "think" – to the subject under investigation, on the basis of publicly observably behavior from the third-person perspective of the interrogator alone. Not straightforward in basic methodology alone, however, the actual ascription of intelligence according to the Turing Test requires no more than an incomplex experimental setting, with the machine and a human being participating in a literal parlor game. Capturing all this in a sentence, we can say that the Turing Test is neither an analysis of linguistic usage nor an apparently opaque phenomenological investigation of an intangible subject matter; rather, it is a simple test of the ability to think, offering an empirical third-person means of ascribing intelligence to the subject under consideration. Yet, as this paper will argue, while Turing's test appears deceptively simple as it is presented in *Computing Machinery and Intelligence*, it rests on a set of formally unstated, yet philosophically very sophisticated, assumptions about minds and machines that later achieved great prominence in the philosophy of mind.

Ironic as it may furthermore seem, Turing's empirical test could have taken its inspiration from a suggestion made by the arch substance dualist in the history of modern philosophy. In his *Discourse on Method*, Descartes raises the possibility of machines being constructed that looked like men, and he mentions two "... very certain means of telling that they were not ... true men." The first means, which may have been a precursor of the Turing Test, rests on the assumption that "they would never use words or other signs, pulling them together as we do in order to tell our thoughts to others."

> For one can well conceive of a machine being so made as to pour forth words, and even words appropriate to the corporeal actions that cause a change in its organs – as, when one touches it in a certain place, it asks what one wants to say to it, or it cries out that it has

been injured, and the like – but *it could never arrange its words differently so as to answer to the sense of all that is said in its presence*, which is something even the most backward men can to.[18]

In *A Philosophicall Discourse Concerning Speech, Conformable to the Cartesian Principles* from 1668, Cartesian Géraud de Cordemoy similarly argues about parrots and "other bodies, whose figure is very different from [his own]", that:

> ...I think I may... establish for a Principle, [t]hat... if I finde by all the Experiments, I am capable to make, that they use speech as I do, I shall think, I have infallible reason to believe they have a soul as I.[19]

Simply put, the Turing Test is a formally structured test of ascertaining whether the machine can "arrange its words differently so as to answer to the sense of all that is said in its presence" or "use speech" as we do. The major difference between the Cartesian test and the Turing Test, is that the latter requires a physical interrogator-participant separation. We can refer to this separation as the delineation of the interrogator's *domain of investigation* – i.e. as the circumscription to text-only conversation of the expanse of facts about the participants in a Turing Test that the interrogator is permitted to probe.

As Turing argues:

> We do not wish to penalise the machine for its inability to shine in beauty competitions, nor to penalise a man for losing in a race against an aeroplane. The conditions of our game make these disabilities irrelevant.[20]

The assumption behind this, is that something that is capable of passing a test of linguistic competence, also would be able to perform a whole range of other clearly intelligent actions – that linguistic competence, inspected within an appropriately delineated domain of investigation by the question and answer method, can reveal all the data required for the ascription of intelligence.

> The question and answer method seems to be suitable for introducing almost any one of the fields of human endeavour that we wish to include.[21]

Not only does the Turing Test screen off the physical appearance of the participants, however – it also screens off all other facts outside the purlieu of its domain of investigation. Since the interrogator is unable to directly perceive the participants in any manner, and since he is provided no background information about them either – including information about their past history (whether they were born by human beings or constructed in a workshop) and information about their internal workings (whether they consist of biological organs or electronic components) – the participants can in principle have *any past history* and *any internal workings* imaginable and still be regarded as intelligent beings, provided they are not disrobed by a lack of linguistic competence.[22]

Within the Turing Test's domain of investigation, on the other hand, the interrogator is to make full use of his probative power, having received carte blanche to employ whatever strategy (or stratagem) he deems useful for achieving the aim of unmasking the participants. His questions might include current political events in the Middle East, the interpretation of Byronic poetry, humorous stories, or even the issue of appropriate funeral etiquette.

Closely related to the issue of the test's domain of investigation is the issue of its *criterion of success* – the question of when the requirements of the test can indeed be said to have been satisfied. Throughout the first part of *Computing Machinery and Intelligence* Turing does not provide a clear specification of this criterion – he merely mentions, for example, the possibility of the interrogator deciding wrongly "as often" in the machine imitation game as he does during the male-female imitation game. He similarly mentions the possibility of the machine playing the imitation game "*satisfactorily*". Finally, however, he says:

> ...we are not asking whether all digital computers at present available would *do well* [in the imitation game], but whether there are imaginable computers which would *do well*.[23]

In the most generalized terms, then, we can say that the participant meets the Turing Test criterion of success when he/she/it *does well in the imitation game*. To "do well", however, is still too amphibological a term to constitute a precise criterion of success. In fact, the question "Has the participant done well in the Turing Test?" is no less ambiguous than the original question, "Can machines think?" – resultantly procuring mere obscurum per obscurius. Apparently aware of this, Turing offers a specific prediction in the sixth subsection of *Computing Machinery and Intelligence* that has subsequently been interpreted as the criterion of success for his test:

> I believe that in about fifty years' time it will be possible to programme computers, with a storage capacity of 10^9, to make them play the imitation game so well that an average interrogator will not have more than 70 per cent chance of making the right identification after five minutes of questioning.[24]

And:

> I believe that at the end of the century the use of words and general educated opinion will have altered so much that one will be able to speak of machines thinking without expecting to be contradicted.[25]

So, although Turing regards the original question "Can machines think?" to be "too meaningless to deserve discussion", he predicts that a 70% detection rate by the interrogators will coincide around the year 2000 with the general acceptance of machine thinking – a projected general acceptance he nowhere voices disagreement with. Since the storage capacity of the machine clearly is inscrutable to the interrogator, we are left with the predicted 70% detection rate as our guideline for the criterion of success. If the interrogator is to have a detection rate of 70%, the computer must have a deception rate of 30%, and since this is to be assessed after 5 minutes of questioning, we can refer to this as the *30/5 criterion*. This criterion should not, of course, be interpreted as an essentialist definition of machine intelligence, according to which intelligence arises in machines that satisfy it like some Bergsonesque élan vital – it should, rather, be understood as a stipulation of a sufficient criterion for intelligence ascription that Turing certainly regarded as demanding enough. In fact, he is merely concerned with the possibility that the intelligence-ascription bar may be *too high* – not about the possibility that it might have been set too low.

> The game may perhaps be criticised on the ground *the odds are weighted too heavily against the machine.*[26]

It is to the very issue of whether the Turing Test's criterion of success is too difficult or too easy to satisfy – to the issue of whether the test is over- or underconstrained – that the main arguments raised against it appertain. French, for example, has argued by reference to a subcognitive question strategy that the test is overconstrained – while Searle's well-known Chinese Room Argument lends support to the contention that the test is underconstrained, inasmuch as it can in principle be passed by a mere Chinese Room syntax-manipulator.

This outlines the domain of investigation and the criterion of success of the test, but still leaves unanswered two important interpretational issues concerning the test:

1. The "level" of thinking ascribed by the Turing Test (III).
2. The status of Turing's prediction (IV).

III. The Level of Thinking Ascribed by the Test

Let us assume, then, that a hypothesized machine fulfills the 30/5 criterion, co-inciding with the predicted general acceptance of machine thinking, and so enabling "one to speak of machines thinking without expecting to be contradicted" as Turing put it. What will this "thinking", about which one can speak without expecting to be contradicted, amount to? Will it be akin to the low-level mental phenomena assumed to be experienced by insects, fish and the like? Or, will it perhaps be akin to the more advanced mental phenomena of squirrels, dogs, cats and the lower primates? Will it conceivably be on a par with the mental phenomena of human beings – or even that of imaginable super-humans? Although we may never know what it is like to be a bat – or a machine capable of satisfying the 30/5 criterion (if there is, indeed, anything it is to be this latter) – it is nevertheless important to consider what Turing assumed machine intelligence to amount to. To see this, let us posit for a moment that the intelligence of a machine passing the 30/5 criterion need not surpass the level of the most elementary mentality, found in the most primitive organism of the biological world said to be "intelligent" or to "think" in some vague sense of those words. In such a case, machine intelligence would mean very little. Machines would presumably still be several million years of evolution from exhibiting the intelligence of a common rat, and the ascertainment of their rudimentary mentality would hardly be of anything but purely academic interest – portending no substantial consequences in the foreseeable future for human life, human society or human-machine relations. Let us call this *the subhuman thinking interpretation* of the Turing Test. If, on the other hand, the Turing Test ascertained the presence of a capacity to think in the machine that is akin to human intelligence, machine intelligence would be of great consequence. The advent of a new race of manufactured non-biological intelligent beings would fundamentally change human life and the structure of human society – e.g. by the promise of an endless supply of tireless robot workers, soldiers, scientists and philosophers to do our bidding, or by the threat of intelligent and practically deathless machine enemies – and it would raise profound ethical challenges concerning human-machine interaction, including the issue of machine morality and automaton rights. It would raise, in other words, the sort of issues explored endlessly in science fiction works from Capek's *RUR* and Lang's *Metropolis*, over Asimov's *I, Robot*, to Scott's *Blade Runner*, Gibson's *Neuromancer*, up to the Matrix trilogy by the Wachowski brothers, and beyond. Let us call the view that machines passing the 30/5 criterion should be said to think as well as a human being *the anthropocognate thinking interpretation* of the Turing Test.

Despite the considerable consequences for the interpretation of the Turing Test of clearly establishing the strength of its claim, there nevertheless exists some exegetical disagreement in the Turing Test debate on this very issue. This is well exemplified by the following exchange between two leading figures. In his 1990 contribution to *Mind*,[27] French assumes that the nature of the "thinking" or the "intelligence" ascribed by Turing to machines passing the Turing Test is one comparable to human intelligence. Relying on this assumption, he criticizes Turing for not taking into account the intelligence of non-human animals. This interpretation subsequently drew fire from Michie in the paper *Turing's Test and Conscious Thought*, published by the journal *Artificial Intelligence*, where the he writes:

> We have to remind ourselves that – in spite of subsequent misstatements, repeated and amplified in a recent contribution to *Mind* by Robert French – the question which Turing wished to place beyond reasonable dispute was *not* whether a machine might think at the level of an intelligent human. His proposal was for a test of whether a machine could be said to think at all.[28]

Framing the French-Michie disagreement in the terms introduced so far, we can say that French assumes the anthropocognate thinking interpretation of the Turing Test, while Michie criticizes him from the standpoint of the subhuman thinking interpretation of the test.

Which interpretation should we prefer? In short, we should prefer the anthropocognate thinking interpretation – Michie's criticism to the contrary notwithstanding – since it is the one most strongly supported by the complete extant textual evidence, including the evidence provided by Turing's personal notes. As revealed by this surprisingly overlooked material, Turing makes a number of statements in support of a strong interpretation of the cognitive level attributable to machine intelligence. For example:

> ... I believe that the attempt to make a thinking machine will help us greatly in finding out how we think ourselves. [29]
>
> "You cannot make a machine to think for you". This is a commonplace that is usually accepted without question. It will be the purpose of this paper to question it.[30]

Clearly, if machines aid us in finding out how we ourselves think, and if they will come to be able to "think for [us]", they will have to exhibit a level of cognitive functioning at least akin to ours. Indeed, according to Turing, there is no human characteristic insusceptible to machine imitation:

> It is customary, in a talk or article on this subject, to offer a grain of comfort, in the form of a statement that some particular human characteristic could never be imitated by a machine. It might for instance be said that no machine could write good English, or that it could not be influenced by sex-appeal or smoke a pipe. I cannot offer any such comfort, for I believe that no such bounds can be set.[31]

Not only does this statement support the anthropocognate thinking interpretation, but additional evidence actually points to an even stronger claim on Turing's part:

> Let us now assume, for the sake of argument, that these machines are a genuine possibility, and look at the consequences of constructing them... There would be great opposition from the intellectuals who were afraid of being put out of a job. It is probable though that the intellectuals would be mistaken about this. There would be plenty to do, i.e. in trying to keep ones intelligence up to the standard set by the machine, *for it seems probable that once the machine thinking method has started, it would not take long to outstrip our feeble powers.* There would be no question of the machines dying, and they would be able to converse with each other to sharpen their wits. At some stage therefore we should have to expect machines to take control, in the way that is mentioned in Samuel Butler's Erewhon'.[32]

Butler's famous satire *Erewhon* mentions machines taking control in the following manner:

> I learned that about four hundred years previously, the state of mechanical knowledge was far beyond our own, and was advancing with prodigious rapidity, until one of the most learned professors of hypothetics wrote an extraordinary book... proving that the machines were ultimately destined to supplant the race of man, and to become instinct with a vitality as different from, and superior to, that of animals, as animals to vegetable life.[33]

In the statement referring to *Erewhon*, Turing is flirting with the very strong view that machine intelligence would be superior to human intelligence – becoming to us, in Erewhonian terms, as animals to vegetable life. To interpret the Turing Test as claiming to establish the presence of such an intelligence, which would outstrip our feeble powers and make the intellectuals fear unemployment, is to make what we can call *the suprahuman thinking interpretation* of the Turing Test. Of the three interpretations – the subhuman, the anthropocognate and the suprahuman – the subhuman is clearly inadequate in light of the adjuvant textual evidence from Turing's notes. Furthermore, if the Turing Test was only formulated to establish the presence of the ability to do "thinking as such", i.e. if it was only formulated to establish the presence of some vaguely defined mental capacity supposedly possessed by all beings who are in some way said to "think", from the rat to the philosopher – it obviously is guilty of utter overconstrainment, a point Turing hardly could have so blithely overlooked. After all, beings such as cats, dogs and chimpanzees, whose ability to think in some sense of that term is all but irrefragable today – could never pass such a test. Only human beings, or beings with the ability to do at least not too inferior a kind of thinking, could be expected to use language well enough to pass it. Yet, even given this, it is still debatable whether Turing's view is best captured by the anthropocognate thinking interpretation or by the suprahuman thinking interpretation.

The problem is as follows. On the one hand, why would a thinking machine "help us greatly in finding out how we think ourselves", if it performed something substantially different from, and superior to, our form of thinking? Analogously, a study of distinctively human thinking (e.g. a study of concepts, generalizations, propositions, induction and deduction) would be rather unhelpful, if our aim was to understand the mentality of a rat or pigeon – and so it seems that the man-machine difference cannot be similarly chasmal. On the other hand, how can we maintain that machine intelligence is really like our own, if it is conducted by tireless, unerring and virtually deathless non-biological beings who are as superior to us as animal life is to vegetable life? This is a conundrum to be sure, with the former consideration lending support to the anthropocognate thinking interpretation, and the latter lending support to the suprahuman thinking interpretation. Fortunately we need not unequivocally favor either of those. A sufficient interim interpretation – which we may call *the open-ended anthropocognate thinking interpretation* – will suffice for our purposes. According to this interpretation, the Turing Test maintains that the machine that satisfies the 30/5 criterion will be said to think *at least as well as* a human being.

In brief, the advantage of this interpretation is that it can be fully integrated with all of Turing's statements about machine mentality, while not being subject to the risk inherent in the suprahuman thinking interpretation of ascribing to Turing an unfairly strong claim. Consequently, we maintain that the thinking ascribed by the Turing Test to the successful candidate can be no less than human-level, but at the same time we abstain from specifying exactly how great the level of thinking is said to be.

IV. Turing's Predictions

Having introduced evidence in support of the open-ended anthropocognate thinking interpretation, we should now take a moment to assess Turing's prediction of the three interrelated conditions that would obtain at about the year 2000 – a prediction, as we saw in section II, that is intimately connected with the 30/5 criterion.

The prediction contains the following main elements:

1. Computers with a storage capacity of 10^9 will exist.
2. The general educated opinion will have altered so much that one will be able to speak of machine thinking without expecting to be contradicted.
3. The 30/5 criterion will be passed.

Let us briefly consider each in turn:

1. Computers with a storage capacity of 10^9 exist. This prediction of Turing's has been lauded as amazingly accurate, since a new mid-range home PC in the year 2000 had a storage capacity of approximately 10 gigabytes, equal to about 10^{10} bytes. The defect of the lauding is that it relies upon the mistaken assumption that Turing was predicting the storage capacity of a mid-range home PC. In fact, what is generally viewed as the first PCs or home computers were introduced in the 1970's, long after Turing's death in 1954. Turing himself worked on the Manchester Mark 1, the first commercially manufactured electronic stored-program computer, build in collaboration between the University of Manchester and the Manchester firm Ferranti Ltd. At the time when Turing wrote *Computing Machinery and Intelligence*, only three computers were in ex-

istence besides the Mark 1 – the Cambridge EDSAC, and the American ENIAC and BINAC. A late 20ᵗʰ century ectype of the Mark 1 – which was a vast installation with two bays measuring 16 by 8 by 4 feet – is not a home PC, mid-range or otherwise, but rather a commercial installation such as a so-called "server-farm" (an interconnected installation of servers in which large amounts of data can be stored and accessed) or a "supercomputer" (an ultra high-speed parallel computing system). Individual units of server-farms easily boasts storage capacity of terabyte-proportions – and so, computer installations exist today, as they did in 2000, that have many thousand times the storage capacity predicted by Turing. The increase in capacity, however, has not been limited to storage alone. Current supercomputers, consisting of hundreds of computers connected by a high-speed network, are able to attain an execution performance speed into the trillions of floating-point operations per second – easily outstripping by the millionfold the speed of the Mark 1, regarded by Turing as probably sufficient for machine intelligence.[34] In sum, Turing should not be said to have accurately predicted – nor even to have envisioned – the immense calculating power of computers in the year 2000. Of course, hardly anybody could have predicted the exponential fin de siècle improvement in information technology, and Turing's prediction about the year 2000 level of calculating power surely appeared outrageously optimistic at the time when he made it. What is important to keep in mind, however, is that the Technological Insufficiency Reply in defense of the Turing Test, which employs the strategy of arguing that the level of computing power required by the Turing Test isn't here yet, but that it surely will be in another 10, 20 or n years – is branded with a prima facie implausibility, since we already have exceeded Turing's own expectations by a near astronomical margin.

2. The general educated opinion in favor of machine thinking. According to Turing, the general educated opinion will have altered so much by the year 2000 that one will be able to speak of machine thinking without expecting to be contradicted. Certainly, this prediction about the *general* educated opinion must be characterized as mistaken. Today it is still a highly debatable issue and one certainly should presume to be contradicted – often and vehemently – if one argues for machine thinking. For confirmation of this, one need merely inquire about the opinion on the matter held by a random selection of one's friends, family and acquaintances, while keeping in mind the open-ended anthropocognate thinking interpretation of the Turing Test – i.e. while keeping in mind that the machine thinking meant by Turing is thinking at least on the lev-

el of a human being. Concerning the *specialized* educated opinion – the opinion among artificial intelligence researchers – the case is somewhat less homologous. As Searle describes the views of the well-known the founders of classical artificial intelligence in his 1984 Reith Lectures:

> Herbert Simon of Carnegie-Mellon University says that we already have machines that can literally think. There is no question of waiting for some future machine, because existing digital computers already have thoughts in exactly the same sense that you and I do. [35]
>
> Simon's colleague Alan Newell claims that we have now discovered... that intelligence is just a matter of physical symbol manipulation...[36]

Searle continues:

> Marvin Minsky of MIT says that the next generation of computers will be so intelligent that we will 'be lucky if they are willing to keep us around the house as household pets'.[37]
>
> ...John McCarthy, the inventor of the term 'artificial intelligence'... says even 'machines as simple as thermostats can be said to have beliefs'. And indeed, according to him, almost any machine capable of problem-solving can be said to have beliefs.[38]

This being noted, however, the correctness or incorrectness of Turing's sociological prediction about widespread opinions is an issue separate from that of the validity of his test – and thus lends decisive support to neither defenders nor detractors of the test.

3. The 30/5 criterion will be passed. At this point, well after the year 2000, the Turing Test has yet to be passed by a machine – and based on a projection from the current state of affairs, it is not likely to happen in the near future either. A measure of the current status of Turing Test programming is the performance of the contestants at the aforementioned Loebner Prize Contest. Despite both the high-profile nature of the test and the alluring prize money, no computer has been brought close to passing the 30/5 criterion so far. As a behind-the-scenes observer at the 2003 contest, and judging by the quality of the artificial intelligence programs I witnessed, I find it quite safe to predict that the 30/5 criterion – if applied rigorously according to Turing's prescriptions – will not be met by a machine in the near future, and perhaps not even within the next 10, 15 or 25 years. Still, it appears to be an in-principle empirical possibility that a machine will eventually pass the Turing Test. For our present purposes, however, it simply suffices to observe that Turing indeed overestimated the ability of machines to pass the 30/5 criterion by the year 2000.

In sum, Turing's prediction of the three interrelated conditions that would obtain at about the year 2000 must be deemed mistaken. As we have noted, computers with a storage capacity of proportions far greater than 10^9 are readily available – yet the general educated opinion does not affirm the existence of machine thinking and the 30/5 criterion has so far remained unmet.

So, having examined and interpreted the Turing Test *superstructure* – the specific nature and claims of the test itself – let us now turn to the key assumptions concerning minds and machines underlying the test – the *substructure* of the test, as it were.

V. Turing Mechanism and Discrete State Machines

In this section, I will examine Turing's view of the nature of machines – including his cornerstone concept of the universal machine (V and VI). Proceeding from this, I will argue that a key philosophical assumption of Turing's is a doctrine I have termed Turing mechanism, according to which human beings are machines through and through and the human mind can be understood in strictly functional and mechanistic terms (VII and VIII). I will furthermore argue that the Turing Test significantly hinges on this doctrine, and that Turing's otherwise puzzling employment of an imitation game as the standard for the ascription of machine intelligence, only can be fully understood in the light of such a mental ontology (VIII). Finally, I will relate Turing mechanism to a wider context in the philosophy of mind (IX). I have relied heavily on Turing's personal notes in this undertaking.

Let us start by examining Turing's view on the nature of machines. Specifically, we must examine his view on the nature of discrete state machines, universal machines and digital computers.

Discrete state machines are machines that move in separate states from one position to another with no intermediate states. As a simple example, imagine a cogwheel whose individual states are defined by the position of an opposed toothed mechanism in the space between two teeth of the wheel. Changes in the individual states occur as the toothed mechanism moves to the next space between two teeth on our cogwheel. With no intermediate positions, the total number of states is a finite sum determined by the number of teeth – and this mechanism, where movement from one definite state to another occurs as a sudden jump or click, can therefore be regarded as a discrete state machine.

[D]iscrete state machines... are the machines which move by sudden jumps or clicks from one quite definite state to another. These states are sufficiently different for the possibility of confusion between them to be ignored.[39]

In the strictest sense there really are no such machines. To see this, simply imagine subjecting our cogwheel mechanism to a more thorough examination. While the movement from one definite state on the wheel to another at first appears to occur as a sudden jump or definite click, slow motion video footage, for example, would reveal that it really is a continuous process. Viewing such footage, we would see that the toothed mechanism smoothly traverses the entire distance between the definite state spaces, eventually settling down in a new space. Nevertheless, the strict impossibility of discrete state machines aside, according to Turing, many kinds of machine can profitably be thought of as discrete:

Strictly speaking there are no such machines. Everything really moves continuously. But there are many kinds of machines which can profitably be *thought of* as being discrete state machines... There must be intermediate positions, but for most purposes we can forget about them.[40]

Provided with accurate information about their internal constitution, discrete state machines are in principle predictable: If we know the initial state and the input received by the mechanism, the end state – the discrete state arrived at after a definite series of states – is computable as a determined product thereof (assuming, of course, that the discrete state machine has a finite number of possible states). In other words, if we know that our cogwheel initially is in state 22, that it has 100 states, and that it will receive an input of 10 clockwise clicks by the opposing toothed mechanism, we can predict that it will be in state 32 by the end of the process.

It will seem that given the initial state of the machine and the input signals it is always possible to predict all future states... Even when we consider the actual physical machines instead of the idealised machines, reasonably accurate knowledge of the state at any moment yields reasonably accurate knowledge any number of steps later... *Given the table corresponding to a discrete state machine it is possible to predict what it will do.*[41]

Given the in-principle predictability of discrete state machines, a more general machine could conceivably mimic their behavior by foreseeing and emulating their actions. To understand Turing's view of the nature of such a device, we must now briefly turn to the well-known concept of a Turing machine.

VI. The Turing Machine

Turing presents his eponymous theoretical machine in the paper *On Computable Numbers with an Application to the Entscheidungsproblem*, published in *Proceeding of the London Mathematical Society* in 1936. The problem tackled by Turing – the Entscheidungsproblem – is the question pertaining to a system of symbolic logic, of whether there exists an *effective method* that in principle can be applied to any given expression to decide whether that expression is provable in that system. Turing begins the paper by framing the problem not in terms of proofs, but in terms of computable numbers – the real numbers whose expression as decimals are calculable by finite means – which he, in turn, proceeds to define as the numbers whose decimal can be written down by a machine.[42] A computable number, in other words, is a number capable of being calculated by a Turing machine – an idealized calculating agent, capable of a finite number of conditions ("m-configurations") and supplied with an infinite tape running through it, divided into sections, each capable of bearing a symbol. At any particular moment there is just one square, the "scanned square", in the machine, this constituting the only square of which the machine is "directly aware."[43] The possible behavior of the machine is fully determined by the finite m-conditions along with the scanned symbol – the set of m-conditions constituting the *machine table*. According to its configuration, the machine is capable of performing the following four operations:

1. Write down a new symbol in a blank scanned square (some of which will be part of the solution to the computation being performed, others merely notes to "assist the memory", as Turing put it).
2. Erase the symbol in a non-blank scanned square.
3. Change the square being scanned by shifting one place to the right or left.
4. Change m-configuration.[44]

It was Turing's contention, that these operations include all those that are used in the computation of a number.

The nature of the machine is thus as follows:

I. At any time, the machine is in one of its m-configuration conditions (*mcc*) and a particular square is currently the scanned square (*ss*).
II. What the machine does (*d*) at any specific time (*t*) is completely determined by *mcc* and *ss*, while *d* is limited to the following:

i.   The machine prints a symbol in a blank square, the machine erases a symbol in a non-blank square or the machine erases and prints a symbol in a non-blank square.

ii. The machine changes *ss* at *t* by making the square to the immediate left or right *ss* at t+1.

iii. The machine changes from one *mcc* to another.

iv. The machine halts.

As Turing argued, sufficiently sophisticated machine tables will enable the machine to calculate *any* computable number – and so, he seemed to have further held, also with regard to the behavior of a discrete state machines, which can be mimicked by the Turing machine. A Turing machine, in other words, is a *universal machine* – a machine that is capable of performing the operations of a discrete state machine by imitating its function. To grasp this idea, imagine that Vaucanson or some skilled builder of automatons constructs a mechanical abacus consisting of levers, pulleys and assorted clockwork mechanics. Let us say that the abacus is of labyrinthine complexity with countless different cogwheels turning when two large numbers are added. Let us say, furthermore, that the abacus is so complex that it is capable of adding whole numbers up to 10^{100}. Turing's point would be that however complex, Vaucanson's abacus is still a discrete state machine with a fixed number of operations performed in a certain order, involving a finite number of internal states. As such, we would be able to express its operations in the abstract form of a machine table capable of being implemented by a Turing machine – in turn enabling the latter to functionally mimic the abacus' mechanical sequences of cogwheels moving and numbers being added. While the abacus can only add, the Turing machine – provided with a machine table appropriate to the task – can add, subtract, divide and multiply any computable number, and it can also find astronomically large prime numbers, prove theorems and so on, for any computable set of discrete state operations. By performing computing operations according to the programming of its machine table, the Turing machine can thus predict and imitate the function of any given discrete state machine – and, indeed, it is the very ability to perform such operations on any finite and formal computable content that is the source of power for this device. In accordance with this idea, modern digital computers operate by encoding information into binary code, translating the encoded information into electrical impulses and processing the information according to the rules of a program. Digital computers are thus also universal machines, in Turing's view similarly capable of mimicking the behavior of discrete state machines.

> There is no reason why this calculation [i.e. the prediction of the discrete state machine] should not be carried out by means of a digital computer. Provided it could be carried out sufficiently quickly *the digital computer could mimic the behavior of any discrete state machine...* This special property of digital computers, that they can mimic any discrete state machine, is described by saying that they are *universal* machines.[45]

(As an aside, it should be mentioned that Putnam uses the idea of a Probabilistic Automaton as well as that of a Turing machine in his doctrine of machine functionalism (discussed in the next section). A probabilistic automaton simply is a generalized Turing machine whose machine table includes instructions associated with finite positive probabilities less than or equal to one. As will become clear as we proceed, it makes no difference for the purposes of this paper, whether one's conception of a universal machine is that of a Probabilistic Automaton or that of a Turing machine. For the sake of simplicity, we shall continue to explicate the issue in terms of a Turing machine, as Turing himself did.)

Applied to the problem at hand – the Entscheidungsproblem – Turing's 1936 article answers in the negative that the problem is provably unsolvable. In short, the unsolvability is shown by what has subsequently become known as the *halting problem* – the impossibility for a Turing machine of determining in advance whether a particular algorithm, when executed, will halt or continue perpetually without halting. Of substantial importance to the philosophy of mind, however, was not Turing's particular answer to this problem – a problem of pure mathematics to which Church had already suggested a solution – rather, what was important was Turing's extensive conception of the computable and his idea of a universal machine.

VII. The Nature of the Brain and the Mind

Having discussed Turing's view of discrete state and universal machines, we can proceed with our analysis of his view of the mind. First, let us consider the human brain. This organ, according to Turing, can be viewed as a discrete state machine:

We shall mainly be concerned with *discrete controlling machinery*. As we have mentioned brains very nearly fell into this class, and there seems every reason to believe that they could have been made to fall genuinely into it without any change in their essential properties.[46]

A machine is discrete, "when it is natural to describe its possible states as a discrete set, the motion of the machine occurring by jumping from one state to another."[47] A machine is controlling, "if it only deals with information."[48] A discrete controlling machine – the kind of machine that the brain essentially is – is thus also a discrete state machine, the kind of machine that can be viewed as moving from one position to another without any intermediate states. Since digital computers, qua universal machines, are able to imitate discrete state machines, they are also able to imitate the assumed machine-like functions of the human brain.

If now some particular machine can be described as a brain we have only to programme our digital computer to imitate it and it will also be a brain. If it is accepted that real brains, as found in animals, and in particular in men, are a sort of machine it will follow that our digital computer suitably programmed, will behave like a brain.[49]

If they are programmed to imitate the human brain, they are also able to imitate the human mind. The mind, according to Turing mechanism, *is* the brain – in the sense that there is nothing to the mind not contained in the discrete state functions (as against the structure) of the brain. This latter point, of course, serves as a linchpin assumption of Turing mechanism. In order to throw adequate light upon this central idea, let us first consult the following analogy.

Consider the simplified case of a mechanical clock with the following distinct sets of states:

1. The hour hand that can be in 12 discrete states.
2. The minute hand that can be in 60 discrete states.

This produces a total of 720 discrete states, each corresponding to one minute of a 12 hour period. Now imagine a different mechanical device which need not look like a clock, since we are here concerned with imitating function, not appearance. It could be a Turing machine or a digital computer, but it could also be an elaborate Rube Goldberg system consisting of cans, ropes and pulleys. The reader can imagine the latter as an integrated serial arrangement of 720 cans consecutively being filled up with water (filling each can takes exactly one minute) resulting in the can changing its discrete state by plunging to the ground, setting off the filling of the next can and so on. Imitating the mechanical clock, our daedal system also cycles through exactly 720 discrete states every 12 hours. Whenever the mechanical clock is in state 12, state 257 or state 639, our system is also in state 12, 257 or 639. Our system thus faultlessly mimics the function of the clock. Can we now argue that "being in state 360" and "showing that it is 6 o'clock" are two entirely disjunctive phenomena?

No. Contradistinctly, "showing that it is 6 o'clock" simply is what we call it when our mechanical clock is in discrete state 360. *There is nothing more to "showing that it is 6 o'clock" than being in state 360.* While our Rube Goldberg system doesn't sport two fancy clock hands to help us tell the time, we can nevertheless tell the time just as adequately by this inelegant device: "State 120 – we'd better hurry to the cafeteria for lunch!" Imitating the discrete states of the mechanical clock is equivalent to imitating its ability to show the time. In the same way, Turing seems to have assumed that imitating the discrete state functions of the brain is equivalent to imitating the mind. That is, he seems to have assumed that there exists an *identity relationship of discrete state brain function to mentality.* For Turing, the latter is merely an inaccurate way of stating the former – like saying that our Rube Goldberg system is able to imitate the "time telling ability" of the clock is a true, if somewhat imprecise way of expressing the fact that it is able to imitate all the discrete states of the clock. Although Turing never offered a formal validation of the assumption – or even stated it explicitly – he did make a few revealing statements referring to the identity relationship assumed to obtain between a mental capability (e.g. the ability to think) and the programmed imitation of the brain – asserting, for example, that the former is simply a *less accurate* way of referring to the latter:

> Naturally enough the inclusion of this random element, whichever technique is used, does not solve our main problem, *how to program a machine to imitate a brain, or as we might say more briefly, if less accurately, to think.*[50]

If the machine's ability to think is a less accurate way of referring to its programmed imitation of the brain's discrete state functions, there must ineluctably obtain an identity relationship of some kind between the two phenomena. This mirrors the relationship between "showing that it is 6 o'clock" and "being in state 360", as discussed in our analogy above – and so bulwarks our contention that Turing seems to have assumed a similar relationship between brain function and mentality. In fact, whether Turing ever considered the assumption explicitly or not, an assumed identity relationship of brain function to mentality serves as a necessary centerpiece to afford the amalgamation of Turing mechanism into an internally coherent doctrine.

Let us now turn to that doctrine.

VIII. Turing Mechanism and the Imitation Game

Turing's view of machine thinking, as we are presently trying to reconstruct it in explicit terms, thus contains the following major points:

1. Discrete state machines are predictable.
2. A universal machine is capable of imitating discrete state machines by mimicking their function.
3. A digital computer is a universal machine.
4. The human brain is a discrete state machine.

From that it follows that a digital computer is capable of imitating the human brain. Now add the further assumption of an identity relationship of brain function to mentality, and we can conclude that a digital computer is capable of imitating the *mind* of a human being. In consequence, we also have an answer in the affirmative to our initial question about machine thinking. We have, in fact, the doctrine of *Turing mechanism*, which states that the human brain can be fully understood as a discrete state machine capable of being imitated by a universal machine, that there exists an identity relationship of brain function to mentality, and that digital computers in principle will be able to think by virtue of their ability to predict and mimic the discrete state functions of the human brain.

If the reasoning in this paper is accepted, this reveals a noteworthy position in the philosophy of mind originated by Turing – an implicitly assumed doctrine of his that can be pieced together from published and unpublished material starting with his introduction of the Turing machine in the 1930's, to his famous formulation of the Turing Test in 1950 and to his last work before his untimely death in 1954.

Benefiting from this explicit formulation of Turing mechanism, we now have a clue to the precise relationship between Turing's mental ontology and his use of the imitation game. In that service, consider my Rube Goldberg system again. Let us say that I am now concerned to answer the question: "can a Rube Goldberg system tell the time?" This question, it seems, is too vague to afford a meaningful answer. After all, various people would regard all sorts of contraptions as "Rube Goldberg systems", and certainly there is no agreement about "telling the time either". Some would regard the Sun as "telling the time" since one can deduce the approximate time from its position, while a Swiss watchmaker might hold that anything not equipped with both a hand-crafted hour and minute hand hardly could be said to tell the time. Attempting to answer the question by means of a Gallup poll – i.e. by means of an average drawn from such partialistic and unscientific views – would clearly be absurd. Let us then simply cut all arguments short by replacing the question with a closely related one, expressed in relatively unambiguous words. In this service, imagine an imitation game played by two devices (operated by their human owners), a wristwatch (A) and a pocket watch (B) and an interrogator (C) who may carry a watch of either type. The interrogator stays in a room apart from the two devices. The object of the game is for the interrogator to determine which is the wristwatch and which is the pocket watch. He knows them by labels X and Y, and at the end of the game he says either 'X is A and Y is B' or 'X is B and Y is A'. The question "can Rube Goldberg systems tell the time", then, will be replaced by the question: what will happen when a Rube Goldberg system takes the part of A in the game? Will the interrogator decide wrongly as often when the game is played like this as he does when the game is played between a wristwatch and a pocket watch?

This, of course, is a close parody of Turing's argument from *Computing Machinery and Intelligence*, simply reframing the issue in terms of the ability of a posited time-telling device to tell the time, rather than in terms of the ability of a machine to think. In my parody, the only question the interrogator could profitably ask is: "what is the time now?"… wait a while… "what is the time now?" – yet, being able to consistently and accurately report the time is *all that we require* for a device to be able to "tell the time". Certainly, our test would take a putative time telling device like the Sun out of the running, since one can only use it to approximately tell the time (and not at all during the night), while my Rube Goldberg system could pass the test since the human operator need merely translate the current state (257) to the corresponding time (17 minutes past 4) and we have a perfectly adequate time telling device. Returning to our discussion, Turing seems to have viewed the machine-man relationship as analogous to the kind of relationship that exists between my Rube Goldberg system and the mechanical clock. In accordance with Turing mechanism, both cases are really instances of a machine to machine comparison (since the brain is assumed to be a discrete state *machine* and the mind is assumed to stand in an identity relationship to its discrete state functions) – and the question of whether one machine is able to do what the other one is able to do, simply reduces to the question of whether we can tell the relevant *function* performed by one apart from the *function* performed by the other. If we cannot, then they should be said to be equivalent in that regard – the Rube Goldberg system should be said to tell the time and machines should be said to think. Following Putnam we can refer to this as a case of *functional isomorphism* – i.e. an instance of the relationship that obtains, if there between two systems is a correspondence between the states of one and the states of the other that preserves functional relations:

> To start with computing machine examples, if the functional relations are just sequence relations, e.g. state A is always followed by state B, then, for F to be a functional isomorphism, it must be the case that state A is followed by state B in system 1 if and only if state F(A) is followed by state F(B) in system 2.[51]

Universal systems, according to Turing mechanism, are thus extraordinarily powerful devices capable of imitating a manifold array of discrete state machines – including human brains and minds. The test of a Turing machine's ability to imitate any particular machine simply reduces to its degree of functional isomorphism with that machine – something that can be impartially established by the *imitation game*. As Turing put it:

> Provided [the calculation] could be carried out sufficiently quickly the digital computer could mimic the behaviour of any discrete state machine. The imitation game could then be played with the machine in question (as B) and the mimicking digital computer (as A) and the interrogator would be unable to distinguish them.[52]

This, then, is the philosophical reasoning that seems to underlie Turing's famous test. Understanding the root of Turing's ideas in his mental ontology, we are thus afforded a deeper understanding of the nature of the imitation game in general and of the Turing Test in particular.

Having identified the doctrine of Turing mechanism, we must now turn to an examination of how it is connected to related views in the philosophy of mind – something that will not only further aid our understanding of the philosophical groundwork of the Turing Test, but also will help us in relating the subsequent critical examination of the test to issues in the basic study of mind wider than merely Turing's doctrine itself.

IX. Turing Mechanism as a Form of Functionalism

To advance our purpose of identifying the exact location of Turing mechanism among related doctrines, let us first very briefly recapitulate the dominant early and mid-20th century views on the fundamental nature of the mind – making our embarkation upon the issue at the point of a major paradigm shift in the field.

Revolting against the late 19th and early 20th century systematic introspective inventorying of the "atomic units" of the human mind by the introspectionists – led by Külpe of the Leipzig school and Titchener of the Cornell school – Watson's *Behaviorism* of 1924 came to serve as the manifesto of a new approach to the study of consciousness. This approach, as is of course familiar by now, consisted in the discarding of direct references to consciousness, and in the almost exclusive concern with the study of behavior. Receiving epistemological assistance from the contemporary surge of positivism and its logical analysis of language – exemplified in the philosophy of mind by Hempel's paper *The Logical Analysis of Psychology* – ontological, logical and methodological behaviorism enjoyed a position of dominance till around 1960, with the publication of such influential monographs as Ryle's *The Concept of Mind* and Skinner's *Science and Human Behavior*. Although by no means removed from the scene overnight (Skinner's *Beyond Freedom and Dignity*, for example, was yet to be published in 1971), behaviorism came to be seriously challenged by the views advanced by Place, Smart and others, according to which reductive identity conditions obtain between mental states and physical states. Known as *identity theory*, this doctrine maintained the strictly intra-agential nature of mental states, reducing those states to neurophysiological ones in accordance with the general program of physicalism. Overpowering both behaviorism and identity theory, however, the theory of functionalism – suggested by Putnam around 1960, most notably with the paper *Minds and Machines* – became the reigning paradigm in the philosophy of mind. Maintaining its regency to the end of the 20th century and arguably still the most widely accepted view of the nature of mind, functionalism, in brief, is the theory that mental states are characterized by the abstract causal roles they play in mediating environmental input and behavioral output; for a state, accordingly, to stand in the right causal relationship to the input and output of an entity, is for that state to be a mental state. Introducing the functionalist doctrine, Putnam argued against both behaviorism and identity theory in what was taken to be a fairly decisive manner. Against behaviorism, Putnam pointed out that our mental states are not simply a cluster of behavioral responses – as illustrated by the imagined case of possible worlds in which pains have unusual responses, as well as possible worlds in which they are not responsible for any responses at all. Exemplifying the latter, Putnam posits the Gedankenexperiment of a community of "super-spartans" in which *all* involuntary pain behavior has successfully been repressed. The relationship between inference about the mental life of a given system on the one hand, and the actual and potential behavior of that system on the other, seems therefore always to be defeasible, belying the behaviorists' exclusive concern with behavior. Against identity theory, Putnam argued that since mental states are to be identified with brain states – e.g. pain being identified with c-fibers firing – the implication is that a given mental state always and everywhere must retain the neurophysiological characterization initially assigned to it. Accordingly, the only way for a given creature to feel pain – a creature of any conceivable species, on earth or of extraterrestrial origin – is for that creature to have c-fibers firing. Yet, Putnam argued, this is an indefensibly arbitrary and narrow conception of pain; an instance of species chauvinism, it would appear. The relationship between inference about the mental life of a given system on the one hand, and the physical composition of that system on the other, therefore also seem to be defeasible – belying the identity theorist's reduction of mental states to physical ones. What was offered by Putnam as an alternative to both of these doctrines, was a theory that – like identity theory – identified mental states as internal states of the organism, yet did so, not in concrete neuroanatomical terms of identity theory, but rather in an abstract manner – i.e. a manner that pertains to the functioning of a thing, not its specific matter.

Returning to Turing mechanism, we can now begin to narrow down the sector in the philosophy of mind topography to which it belongs. To behold this clearly, let us spell out in a little greater detail Putnam's specific doctrine of *machine functionalism*, according to which we are to understand mental states on the paradigm of the machine table states of a Turing machine.[53]

> ...I have argued for the hypothesis that (1) a whole human being is a Turing machine, and (2) that psychological states of a human being are Turing machine states or disjunctions of Turing machine states.[54]

Accordingly, the mental state of pain (Putnam regards "pain" as a stock example of a mind word) is thus simply a functional state of the pain-feeling entity.

> I shall, in short, argue that pain is not a brain state, in the sense of a physical-chemical state of the brain (or even of the whole nervous system), but another *kind* of state entirely. I propose the hypothesis that pain, or the state of being in pain, is a functional state of a whole organism.[55]

For Turing mechanism, as for machine functionalism, the abstract conception of mental states as states capable of being instantiated in beings biologically different from us – and even in entirely non-biological entities like digital computers – is afforded by the abstract nature of the Turing machine. As Putnam explains:

> In particular, the "logical description" of a Turing machine does not include any specification of the *physical nature* of [the] "states" – or indeed, of the physical nature of the whole machine. (Shall it consist of electronic relays, of cardboard, of human clerks sitting at desks, or what?) In other words, a given "Turing machine" is an *abstract* machine which *may be physically realized in an almost infinite number of different ways.*[56]

Nor would the Turing machine, in principle, even need to be a physical machine – provided it was still capable of adequately instantiating the required machine table states.

> Strictly speaking, a Turing Machine need not even be a physical system; anything capable of going through a succession of states in time can be a Turing Machine.[57]

So, it is the abstract nature of the Turing machine – the assumed ability of this universal machine to predict and emulate the function of discrete state machines including human brains – that gives rise to the claim of its in-principle ability to exhibit human mentality. This, in turn, naturally gives rise to the *multiple realizability* view of mental states – i.e. to the assumption that mental properties are realizable by an unspecified range of physical or non-physical systems, alone assuming that those systems exhibits the required functional properties. This implementation-independent view of mentality is one of the chief advantages functionalism is thought to have over physicalist theories, including identity theory – and it is a core contention of the theory itself. Yet, as we saw earlier in this paper, Turing essentially anticipated this view in published and unpublished material dating back to the 1930's and culminating with *Computing Machinery and Intelligence* in 1950. At least a decade before Putnam's introduction of functionalism in circa 1960, then, Turing already assumed a full-fledged functionalist doctrine – a doctrine that included all the key ideas of machine functionalism: the cornerstone concept of the Turing machine, the idea of the abstract functional realization of the "causal role" of mental states on the paradigm of the machine table of a Turing machine, the assumption of the multiple realization of mental states afforded by the abstract nature of the Turing machine and, finally, the "synthesis" (as we may call it) of behaviorism and identity theory, according to which mental states are unmistakably internal states of the entity in question (like identity theory, unlike behaviorism), without, however, simply being reduced to species-specific neurophysiological states (like behaviorism, unlike identity theory).[58] I suggest that this observation constitute grounds for a reconsideration of recent intellectual history in the philosophy of mind, as it suggests that the primogenitureship of the exceedingly influential doctrine of functionalism – by a margin of about a decade – lies not with Putnam but rather with the father of the Turing machine himself.

This brings us to the one noteworthy difference between Turing mechanism and machine functionalism. Having explicitly identified the underlying theory of Turing mechanism (V-VIII), we see that Turing assumed a view of the fundamental nature of mental states – that they are to be understood on the paradigm of machine table states of a Turing machine – in addition to suggesting the imitation game format for the practical ascertainment of the presence of such states (VIII).

Machine functionalism, by contrast, while in agreement with Turing mechanism on the same functionalistic view of the nature of mental states, nevertheless lacks a *practicable procedure* for ascertaining the machine table states of a given system. In other words, it lacks a specific strategy for ascertaining when, in fact, a relationship of psychological isomorphism obtains between two systems.

In general, such a relationship exists, according to Putnam, under the following conditions:

> Thus, to say that a man and a robot have the same 'psychology' (are *psychologically iso-morphic*, as I will also say) is to say that the behavior of the two species is most simply and revealingly analyzed, at the psychological level (in abstraction from the details of the internal physical structure), in terms of the same 'psychological states' and the same hypothetical parameters.[59]

Yet, given the vast number of human mental states and their multitudinary interrelationships i.e., in the terminology of Turing mechanism and machine functionalism, given the vastness of the human machine table – combined with the necessarily inferential nature of our knowledge of that machine table – the identification of isomorphism on the level of particular states seems to be impossible to implement in actual practice. The desire of machine functionalists for such an identification – for an "ideal psychological theory", as Putnam calls it – simply amounts to a form of intellectual nympholepsy. In his later writing, Putnam recognizes this defect:

> Even if we are charitable, we shall have to admit that the 'ideal psychological theory' that I envisaged in my functionalist papers, the kind of theory that could provide as complete a description of our psychological states as a Turing Machine Table provides for the functional states of a computer, is an utterly Utopian project (and if we are uncharitable we will simply say it is a 'we know not what').[60]

Turing's form of functionalism, however, avoids this early Putnamesque utopianism – precisely on account of the Turing Test, which affords Turing a practical procedure for ascertaining the presence of relevant functional isomorphism between the machine tables of two different systems (e.g. between a human being and a machine), without having to perform the utopian task of providing a complete description of the Turing machine table states as in Putnam's ideal psychological theory.

Whether Turing's test is held to be valid or not, this suggests that Turing held an overall functionalist view that was theoretically more comprehensive than Putnam's, at least in this regard. In a statement that comes remarkably close to Turing's position, Putnam concludes the article *Robots: Machines or Artificially Created Life?* published by *The Journal of Philosophy* in 1964, with the contention that the treatment of robots as conscious beings calls for "a decision and not for a discovery" – a decision, at bottom, coming down to the alternative of treating robots as members of our linguistic community, or as machines.[61] This is exactly what the present paper has argued that the Turing Test was intended to provide.

The test was to provide an impartial, empirical and incomplex means of ascertaining whether a given digital computer successfully has imitated the machine table of the human brain, and so also the mind of a human being, and thus could be admitted as a member of our linguistic community.

This brings to a close our major discussion of Turing's underlying philosophical doctrine. Let us now reverse the direction of our trajectory, bringing the weight of the of Turing mechanism to bear upon our topic of the Turing Test, to see how the identification of the former casts further light upon the latter, on at least the following four easily discernable points:

1. As we saw in section II, the domain of investigation specifies that the participating machine in principle can have any past history and any internal workings imaginable and be regarded as intelligent, provided it is not disrobed on the basis of conversational performance. Understanding the substructure, we can appreciate this is an expression of both functionalism (conversational performance, viewed as the input-output data of a Turing machine executing a posited mentality-emulating machine table, is a type of functional performance) and of the assumption of the multiple realizability of mental states (the machine can have any past history and any internal working).

2. As we also saw in section II, the 30/5 criterion that specifies the height of the intelligence-ascription bar, does so in strictly functional terms. The machine must exhibit the ability to deceive at a success rate of 30% after 5 minutes of questioning – deception being the functional ability of programmed machine to mislead the interrogator, by executing one of a potentially unlimited range of mentality-emulating machine tables.

3. As we saw in section III, the open-ended anthropocognate thinking interpretation of the test ascribes at least human-level intelligence to non-human beings, regardless of their species and structural properties – again a position clearly coherent with functionalism and the implementation-independent view of mentality.

4. As we saw in section IV, Turing's own predictions about machine intelligence reveal that he regarded the necessary hardware requirements of the machines as relatively minor by today's standards, while he viewed the programming challenge – the challenge of equipping a digital computer with a functionally adequate machine table for the imitation of human intelligence – as the substantial one.[62]

Thus, having argued for the plausibility of ascribing to Turing the doctrine of Turing mechanism, we have determined that Turing mechanism and machine functionalism are two substantially similar views, that both are genealogical subspecies of functionalism in general (that, indeed, the former appears to be the real primogenitor of functionalism in recent intellectual history), and that both doctrines are inextricably interwreathed with the assumption of the multiple realizability of mental states afforded by the abstract nature of the Turing machine. Furthermore, we discern that Turing mechanism, enjoying the coadjuvancy of the Turing Test, offers more easily realizable practical test of functional isomorphism (the 30/5 criterion within the Turing Test domain of investigation, as we saw in section II) than Putnam's utopian state-to-state "ideal psychological theory" – and thus actually appears to be a more comprehensive overall doctrine. Indeed, we finally noted, the Turing Test predated Putnam's somewhat vague suggestion that the treatment of robots comes down to a decision to allow them membership of our linguistic community, just as the doctrine of Turing mechanism seems to have predated that of machine functionalism.

Notes
1. Moor 2000 (p. 461).
2. French 2000a (p. 2).
3. French 2000b (p. 2).
4. Preston 2002 (p. 7).
5. Hofstadter 1985, Eisner 1991, Jacquette 1993, Korukonda 2002, Searle 2000 and many others, all assume the operational interpretation – while Moor 1976, 1998, 2001 persistently has defended an inductive adequacy interpretation of the test.
6. It has been argued that imitation game should be interpreted in a more narrowly gender-specific way. See Genova 1994, Keith 1994, Sterrett 2000. Convincing criticism of this view has been voiced in Anderson 1994, Piccinini 2000 and Moor 2001.
7. For an introductory overview of the Chinese Room Argument debate, see the 10-page bibliography in Preston and Bishop 2002 (pp. 393-403).
8. Colby et al. 1972, Colby 1981a and 1981b, Heiser et al. 1979, Abelson 1981, Gunderson 1981, Lindsay 1981, Moor 1981 etc.
9. See Watt 1996, Bringsjord 1996, Ford and Hayes 1996 and French 1996.
10. French 1990, 1996, 2000a, 2000b, 2000c and 2001.
11. More than a dozen articles by Harnad are relevant here, but Harnad 1989, 1991, 2000a, 2000b and 2003 are certainly worth mentioning. See also Schweizer 1998.
12. From the 2002 rules. Loebner Prize Contest 2002.
13. Shieber 1994.
14. Jacquette 1993.

15. Turing 1950 (p. 433).
16. Turing 1950 (p. 434).
17. See note 6.
18. Descartes 1993 (p. 32), emphasis added.
19. Cordemoy 1972 (pp. 35-6).
20. Turing 1950 (p. 435).
21. Turing 1950 (p. 435).
22. Turing does limit the "machines" under consideration to electronic or digital computers, and excludes biological beings including "men born in the usual manner". This seems to be a pragmatic limitation on Turing's part, due, perhaps, to the fact that "the present interest in 'thinking machines' has been aroused... [by] the 'electronic computer' or [the] 'digital computer'" as Turing put it. Turing 1950 (pp. 435-6).
23. Turing 1950 (p. 436), emphasis added.
24. Turing 1950 (p. 442).
25. Turing 1950 (p. 442).
26. Turing 1950 (p. 435).
27. French 1990.
28. Michie 1993 (pp. 3-4).
29. Turing 1951c (p. 97).
30. Turing 1951c (p. 96).
31. Turing 1951b (p. 7).
32. Turing 1951b (p. 7), quoted as found in facsimile; emphasis added.
33. Butler 1970 (p. 97).
34. "It is probably not necessary to increase the speed of operations of the machines at all." Turing 1950 (p. 455).
35. Searle 1989 (p. 29).
36. Searle 1989 (p. 29).
37. Searle 1989 (p. 30).
38. Searle 1989 (p. 30).
39. Turing 1950 (p. 439).
40. Turing 1950 (p. 439), emphasis in original.
41. Turing 1950 (pp. 440-1), emphasis added.
42. Turing 1936 (p. 230).
43. Turing 1936 (p. 231).
44. Turing 1936 (pp. 231-2).
45. Turing 1950 (p. 441), emphasis added.
46. Turing 1951a (p. 6), emphasis added.
47. Turing 1951a (p. 5).
48. Turing 1951a (p. 5).
49. Turing 1951b (p. 2),
50. Turing 1951b (p. 5), emphasis added.
51. Putnam 1980a (pp. 134-5).
52. Turing 1950 (p. 441).
53. See Putnam 1980a, 1988, 1996 and 2001. Note that Putnam no longer holds this view.
54. Putnam 1980a (p. 139).
55. Putnam 1980b (p. 226).
56. Putnam 1960 (p. 159), emphasis added.

57. Putnam 1975a (p. 412).

58. One difference between Turing mechanism and machine functionalism is that the former regards the brain as a discrete state machine capable of being imitated by a universal device like a Turing machine, while the latter regards the human brain (or, the whole human organism) as itself a Turing machine.

59. Putnam 1975b (p. 394), emphasis in original.

60. Putnam 2001 (p. 510).

61. Putnam 1975b (p. 406).

62. Turing 1950 (pp. 454-60) and Copeland 1999.

References

Anderson, J. A. 1994. Turing's test and the perils of psychohistory. Social Epistemology, 8.

Abelson, R. P. 1981. Going after PARRY. The Behavioral and Brain Sciences, 4.

Bringsjord, S. 1996. The Inverted Turing Test is Provably Redundant. Psycoloquy, 7.

Butler, S. 1970. Erewhon. Penguin English Library.

Colby, K. M. et al. 1972 Turing-like Indistinguishability Tests for the Validation of a Computer Simulation of Paranoid Processes. Artificial Intelligence, 3.

Colby, K. M. 1981a. Modeling a paranoid mind. The Behavioral and Brain Sciences, 4.

Colby, K. M. 1981b. PARRYing. The Behavioral and Brain Sciences, 4.

Copeland, J. B. 1999. A lecture and two radio broadcasts on machine intelligence by Alan Turing. Machine Intelligence, 15. Proceedings of the Fifteenth Machine Intelligence Workshop, St. Catherine's College, Oxford.

Cordemoy, G. de. 1972. Discourses (1668-70). Scholars' Facsimiles & Reprints.

Descartes, R. 1993. Discourse on Method and Meditations on First Philosophy. Hackett Publishing Company.

Eisner, J. 1991. Cognitive Science And the Search For Intelligence. Invited talk at the Socratic Society.

Ford, K. and Hayes, P. J. 1996. The Turing Test is Just as bad When Inverted. Psycoloquy, 7.

French, R. M. 1990. Subcognition and the limits of the Turing test. Mind, 99.

French, R. M. 1996. The Inverted Turing Test: A Simple (Mindless) Program That Could Pass It. Psycoloquy, 7.

French, R. M. 2000a. The Turing Test: The First Fifty Years. Trends in Cognitive Science, 4. Downloaded from: http://www.ulg.ac.be/cogsci/rfrench/TICS_turing.pdf

French, R. M. 2000b. Peeking Behind the Screen: The Unsuspected Power of the Standard Turing Test. Journal of Theoretical and Experimental Artificial Intelligence, 12.

French, R. M. 2000c. The Chinese Room: Just Say "No!". Proceedings of the 22nd Annual Cognitive Science Society Conference.

French, R. M. 2001. Why Co-Occurrence of Information Alone Is Not Sufficient to Answer Subcognitive Questions. Journal of Theoretical and Experimental Artificial Intelligence, 13.

Genova, J. 1994. Turing's Sexual Guessing Game. Social Epistemology, 8.

Gunderson, K. 1981. Paranoia concerning program-resistant aspects of the mind – and let's drop rocks on Turing's toes again. The Behavioral and Brain Sciences, 4.

Harnad, S. 1989. Minds, Machines and Searle. Journal of Theoretical and Experimental Artificial Intelligence, 1.

Harnad, S. 1991. Other bodies, Other minds: A Machine Incarnation of an Old Philosophical Problem. Minds and Machines, 1.

Harnad, S. 2000a. Minds, Machines and Turing: The Indistinguishability of Indistinguishables. Journal of Logic, Language, and Information (special issue on Alan Turing), 9.

Harnad, S. 2000b. Turing Indistinguishability and the Blind Watchmaker. Evolving Consciousness (Fetzer and Mulhauser eds.). John Benjamins.

Harnad, S. 2003. Can a machine be conscious? How? Journal of Consciousness Studies, 10.

Heiser, J. F.; Colby, K. M.; Faught W. S. et al. 1979. Can Psychiatrists Distinguish a Computer Simulation From the Real Thing? The Limitations of Turing-like Tests as Measure of the Adequacy of Simulations. Journal of Psychiatric Research, 15.

Hofstadter, D. R. 1985. Review of Alan Turing: The Enigma. Metamagical Themas: Questions for the Essence of Mind and Pattern. Penguin Books.

Jacquette, D. 1993. Who's afraid of the Turing Test. Behavior and Philosophy.

Keith, W. 1994. Artificial intelligence, feminist and otherwise. Social Epistemology, 8.

Korukonda, A. R. 2002. Taking stock of Turing test: a review, analysis, and appraisal of issues surrounding thinking machines. International Journal of Human-Computer Studies, 58.

Lindsay, R. 1981. How smart must you be to be crazy? The Behavioral and Brain Sciences, 4.

Loebner Prize Contest. 2002. Loebner Prize Contest Official Rules – Version 2.0.

Michie, D. 1993. Turing's Test and Conscious thought. Artificial Intelligence, 60.

Moor, J. H. 1976. An analysis of Turing's test. Philosophical Studies, 30.

Moor, J. H. 1981. AI and cargo cult science. The Behavioral and Brain Sciences, 4.

Moor, J. H. 1998. Assessing Artificial Intelligence and Its Critics. The Digital Phoenix: How Computers are Changing Philosophy (Bynum and Moor eds.). Blackwell Publishers.

Moor, J. H. 2000. Alan Turing (1912-1954). Minds and Machines, 10.

Moor, J. H. 2001. The Status and Future of the Turing Test. Minds and Machines, 11.

Piccinini, G. 2000. Turing's Rules for the Imitation Game. Minds and Machines, 10.

Preson, J. 2002. Introduction. Views Into the Chinese Room (Preston and Bishop eds.). Oxford University Press.

Preston, J. and Bishop, M. (eds.). 2002. Views Into the Chinese Room. Oxford University Press.

Putnam, H. 1960. Minds and Machines. Dimensions of Mind: A Symposium (Hook ed.). New York University Press.

Putnam, H. 1975a. The mental life of some machines. Mind, Language and Reality. Philosophical papers vol. 2. Cambridge University Press.

Putnam, H. 1975b. Robots: machines or artificially created life? Mind, Language and Reality. Philosophical papers vol. 2. Cambridge University Press.

Putnam, H. 1980a. Philosophy and Our Mental Life. Readings in Philosophy of Psychology vol. 1. (Block ed.). The Language and Thought Series. Harvard University Press.

Putnam, H. 1980b. Brains and Behavior. Readings in Philosophy of Psychology vol. 1. (Block ed.). The Language and Thought Series. Harvard University Press.

Putnam, H. 1988. Why Functionalism Didn't Work. Representation and Reality. MIT Press.

Putnam, H. 1996. Against the New Associationism. Speaking Minds: Interviews with Twenty Eminent Cognitive Scientists (Baumgartner and Payr eds.). Princeton University Press.

Putnam, H. 2001. Putnam, Hilary. A Companion to the Philosophy of Mind (Guttenplan ed.). Blackwell Companions to Philosophy.

Schweizer, Paul. 1998. The Truly Total Turing Test. Minds and Machines 8.

Searle, J. R. 1989a. Minds, Brains and Science. The 1984 Reith Lectures. Penguin Books. Penguin Books.

Searle, J. R. 2000. Minds, Brains, and Programs. Minds, Brains, and Computers (Cummins and Cummins eds.). A Blackwells Philosophy Anthology.

Shieber, S. M. 1994. Lessons from a Restricted Turing Test. Communications of the Association for Computing Machinery, 37.

Sterrett, S. 2000. Turing's Two Tests for Intelligence. Minds and Machines, 10.

Turing, A. M. 1936. On computable numbers, with an application to the Entscheidungsproblem. Proceedings of the London Mathematical Society, 42 (1936-7).

Turing, A. M. 1950. Computing Machinery and Intelligence. Mind: A Quarterly Review of Psychology and Philosophy, LIX.

Turing, A. M. 1951a. Intelligent Machinery. Turing's typed draft. Turing Archive at King's College, Cambridge, CB2 1ST, England.

Turing, A. M. 1951b. Can digital computers think?. Talk broadcast on BBC Third Programme. Turing Archive at King's College, Cambridge, CB2 1ST, England.

Turing, A. M. 1951c. Intelligent machinery, a heretical theory. Lecture given at "'51 Society" in Manchester. Turing Archive at King's College, Cambridge, CB2 1ST, England.

Watt, S. 1996. Naive Psychology and the Inverted Turing Test. Psycoloquy, 7.